Amazon.com
$49.95
P.O. 80142
4-18-02

W9-BZG-804

DISCARDED
Brooks–Cork Library
Shelton State

Liz Winfeld, MA
Susan Spielman, MS

Straight Talk About Gays in the Workplace
Second Edition

*Pre-publication
REVIEWS,
COMMENTARIES,
EVALUATIONS . . .*

"**S** *traight Talk* is just that— straight and to the point. Here's the business case for including sexual orientation as an element of diversity, how it positively impacts your business, how to develop an education and training course to support it, and how to address any concerns about it. As a manager and leader, what more could you want?

Diversity is about valuing individuals. Managing diversity is about eliminating barriers so that you can maximize the contributions of those individuals. Expectations are going up and resources are going down. *Straight Talk* looks at specific strategies for full inclusion in the workplace. As a manager and leader, what more could you ask for?

At Deluxe Corporation, we were able to develop and implement an unprecedented national education and training program on 'Sexual Orientation in the Workplace.' It is because of what we learned in this book and through the collaborative efforts of its authors that we could do this so successfully. I highly recommend it. It's all there. As a manager and leader, what more could you need?"

Rosanne Hastings, MEd
*World Class People Specialist,
Deluxe Corporation*

Brooks - Cork Library
Shelton State
Community College
DISCARDED

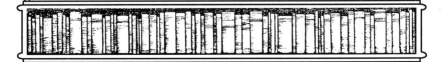

"**A**bout a year ago I was asked to be the 'Executive Champion' of the Ford Motor Company GLOBE (Gay, Lesbian or Bisexual Employees) organization . . . in line with our corporate philosophy of appointing a member of senior management to act as spokesperson or general representative for each of the minority groups that make up our diverse workforce. I was pleased to accept but I was also forthright about my ignorance of the subject. I was fortunate to meet Liz Winfeld shortly after my appointment and I found the first edition of *Straight Talk About Gays in the Workplace* enormously helpful.

The strength of the first book, made even stronger by the updating in the second edition, lies in its no-nonsense, matter-of-fact dealing with the subject in a pragmatic, action-oriented fashion. In a very forthright manner it spells out fact from fiction and outlines some practical action plans for businesses that have to deal with reality, whether they like it or not.

If you need a quick and hard-hitting introduction to this subject, then this is a book I would recommend."

James D. Donaldson
Group Vice President,
Ford Motor Company

"**T**his is a practical book, offering a valuable education in sexual orientation issues as they relate to society and the workplace. Liz Winfeld and Susan Spielman have given us the fullest and most balanced statement of the pros and cons of dealing proactively rather than reactively with full inclusion of sexual orientation, and what we might do to become more effective within our organizations. It is a tribute to the power of the new scholarship about sexual orientation."

Gwen Houston, MS
Vice President of Diversity
and Business Development,
Aetna, Inc.

Harrington Park Press®
An Imprint of The Haworth Press, Inc.

NOTES FOR PROFESSIONAL LIBRARIANS AND LIBRARY USERS

This is an original book title published by Harrington Park Press, an imprint of The Haworth Press, Inc. Unless otherwise noted in specific chapters with attribution, materials in this book have not been previously published elsewhere in any format or language.

CONSERVATION AND PRESERVATION NOTES

All books published by The Haworth Press, Inc. and its imprints are printed on certified pH neutral, acid free book grade paper. This paper meets the minimum requirements of American National Standard for Information Sciences–Permanence of Paper for Printed Material, ANSI Z39.48-1984.

Straight Talk About Gays in the Workplace
Second Edition

HAWORTH Gay & Lesbian Studies
John P. De Cecco, PhD
Editor in Chief

Straight Talk About Gays in the Workplace

Second Edition

Liz Winfeld, MA
Susan Spielman, MS

Harrington Park Press®
An Imprint of The Haworth Press, Inc.
New York • London • Oxford

Published by

Harrington Park Press®, an imprint of The Haworth Press, Inc., 10 Alice Street, Binghamton, NY 13904-1580

© 2001 by Liz Winfeld and Susan Spielman. All rights reserved. No part of this work may be reproduced or utilized in any form or by any means, electronic or mechanical, including photo-copying, microfilm, and recording, or by any information storage and retrieval system, without permission in writing from the publisher. Printed in the United States of America.

Cover design by Monica L. Seifert.

First edition published by the American Management Association, 1995. © Liz Winfeld and Susan Spielman.

Library of Congress Cataloging-in-Publication Data

Winfeld, Liz.
    Straight talk about gays in the workplace / Liz Winfeld and Susan Spielman.—2nd ed.
      p. cm.
    Includes bibliographical references and index.
    ISBN 1-56023-170-X (hard : alk. paper)—ISBN 1-56023-171-8 (soft : alk. paper)
    1. Homosexuality in the workplace. 2. Gays—Employment. 3. Lesbians—Employment. 4. Di-versity in the workplace. 5. Employee fringe benefits. 6. Sexual orientation. I. Spielman, Susan. II. Title.

HD6285 .W56 2000
658.3′0086′64—dc21   00-039712

Much has changed since the first edition of this book came out. What hasn't changed is the love, respect, and gratitude we feel for our parents. We rededicate this book with all that and more to Bev and Sid Winfeld and Amy and Les Spielman, and also in loving memory of Ethel and Morris Moses.

ABOUT THE AUTHORS

Liz Winfeld holds a Master of Arts degree in Education and is a facilitator and writer with extensive experience in both public and corporate education. She is, since the publication of the first edition of *Straight Talk About Gays in the Workplace,* a nationally recognized expert on domestic partner benefits and a much sought-after speaker, facilitator, and curriculum developer of coursework focused on sexual orientation in the workplace.

Sue Spielman holds a Master of Science in Computer Business Management and is an experienced program development manager and curriculum developer. She was the first workplace issues writer for *The Advocate.*

The authors are the principals of *Common Ground,* an education/consulting firm specializing in workplace sexual orientation challenges and domestic partner benefits. They also consult to organizations on the changes—monetary and otherwise—that the legalization of same-sex relationships will mean for business in the United States.

CONTENTS

Acknowledgments

Common Ground, our consulting business, was barely a year old when *Straight Talk About Gays in the Workplace* first appeared. Now its been long enough that we have a seven-year itch to update the book.

In these last six or so years, we have been privileged to work with people in organizations throughout North America, and occasionally from other continents too, to make meaningful workplace education programs on the subject of sexual orientation a reality. We have also made—and are exceedingly proud of—efforts that have led to the successful implementation of domestic partner benefits plans at literally hundreds of organizations. These benefits positively affect the lives of thousands of people . . . regardless of sexual orientation.

We have not done any of this alone, and so thanks are due to all of the employees with whom we have personally worked to engender victories in education and benefits implementation. Remarkable people are putting themselves on the front lines of this battle every day and their efforts do not go unnoticed . . . at least, not by us.

Special thanks to diversity advisory members, employee group members, and HR/diversity management staff at American Express Corporation in Minneapolis, Motorola Corporation in Arizona and Texas, Ford Motor Company in Michigan and beyond, and to everyone involved (especially Rick Schroder) at Shell Oil in Texas and Louisiana. Thanks also to the Deluxe Corporation of Minnesota, especially to Rosanne Hastings, who took a good thing and made it better.

We would also like to acknowledge that the following organizations have made it possible for our work to expand, to improve, and to garner positive results throughout the United States and Canada. They are the U.S. Postal Service, Neiman Marcus, Harcourt General, ERE Yarmouth, Nike, National Geographic, Bellsouth, General Mills, Hewlett-Packard, Disney, the Society for Human Resources Management, the American Management Association, the Honolulu Pacific Federal Executive Board, and last, but certainly not least, Bill Palmer, Melissa Devendorf, and everyone at The Haworth Press who worked with us to bring this second edition out.

Chapter 1

Points of Reference

Certain truths in this life are inescapable. One of them is that humans, as animals and as a race, individually and in groups of varying size, possess certain characteristics that are inherent to their being. Skin color or eye color are examples. This book is about another of those inherent traits.

People who share this trait are not in the majority, which seems to make them automatically suspect and somehow deficient. Estimates of their actual number as a percentage of the world's population usually range from 10 to 20 percent. There is strong evidence that a subset of all other animals also share this characteristic in similar proportions.

Throughout history, people who demonstrate the trait we're discussing have been subject to prejudice, humiliation, discrimination, and negative preconceptions never substantiated by fact. The English words associated with these people are familiar to most, and there are similar words in French, German, Spanish, Latin, Russian, Polish, and just about every other language. Almost without exception, the words are derogatory in nature and in origin.

Religion and superstition in particular have both been extremely hard on this type of person for centuries. These people have been, and in some cases still are, called the devil incarnate, responsible for everything from natural disasters to devastating diseases. In many of the books of the Bible, they are singled out as the personification of evil and contrary to everything that is holy and sacrosanct.

The authors of this book share this trait, and as such bear part of the burden foisted on us by others who are hateful or fearful or just honestly ignorant of the facts. People tried to change us when we were younger because they thought we chose to be as we are and that a life lived by people such as us is much harder in all ways. People such as us are likely to die nine years sooner than other types of people. We are more likely to develop diabetes, epilepsy, thyroid problems, sleep disorders, and autoimmune illnesses. We are women who, with others like us, must daily call upon our ingenuity to deal with a world not designed for our kind, and who must also on a daily basis find the courage to confront societal inequities and bias by stating simply that, despite all the difficulties, we are proud to be le . . . ft-handed.

Bet you thought we would write something else, right? That we are proud to be l . . . iberals? We are. That we are delighted to be Le . . . os? Liz is in fact a Leo (Sue's a Virgo in case you are interested). No. You probably thought we were going to say that we are proud to be lesbians, and in fact, that would be true too. But you will not hear either of us use that particular word. We'll get back to that in a moment. But, first, we have this left-handed thing to explore.

The English word *left* is derived, as is so much of English, from the Anglo-Saxon. The Anglo-Saxon word for *left* is *lyft,* which means "weak" or "broken." The *Oxford English Dictionary* defines *left-handed* as "crippled, defective, inept, characterized by underhanded dealings, ill-omened, and illegitimate." In French, the word for *left* is *gauche,* which means "crooked" and "uncouth." In German, it's *linkisch,* which means "clumsy" and "maladroit." Italians say *mancino,* which comes from *mancus,* meaning "crooked, maimed, dishonest, and deceitful." And in Latin, the word for *left* is *sinister,* from *sinistrum,* which means "evil."

Among superstitious people, left-handedness is not a positive attribute. In Scotland, in Morocco, among gypsies, and in parts of North America, if your right palm itches, it is said you will soon receive money. But if it's your left palm, you are certain to lose money. In North Africa, if your right eye twitches, you will be reunited with someone you love; twitches in your left eye signify that someone close to you is going to die. And why do we throw salt over our left shoulders? Because it is over the left shoulder that the devil is said to lurk. Furthermore, check any depiction of Satan in books or on tarot cards, and you'll see that he is most decidedly left-handed.

In Judeo-Christian tradition, right is always good and left is always bad. In the Old Testament, in Leviticus, for example, left-handedness is singled out as a "blemish" a priest cannot have. And in the Roman Catholic, Eastern Orthodox, Lutheran, and Anglican churches of Christianity, all rites are performed with the right hand. To do so with the left is considered very unlucky. Finally, the Bible tells us that the thief crucified with Christ to his right ascended to heaven, while the thief on Jesus' left descended to hell.[1]

Another parallel between sexual orientation and handedness is worth considering. That parallel lies in the statistic (using very general percentages) that 80 percent of all humanity is right-handed (left-brained); 15 percent is left-handed (right-brained); and the remainder is ambidextrous. Also, the evidence seems to conclude that 80 percent of humanity is predominantly heterosexual; 15 percent is predominantly homosexual; 2 to 3 percent is predominantly bisexual; and the remainder is predominantly asexual. The use of the word *predominantly* is purposeful; as we'll see in a moment, there is little about the human animal that is absolute.

What do these percentages signify? We have always found it interesting that being in the majority seems to equal being in the right. In other words, if most people are right-handed then it must be the right way to be. If most people are heterosexual, it must be the right way to be. If you also happen to think that comparisons between these two traits— and the importance assigned them by so many—is at the same time compelling and ultimately ridiculous, then you are certainly not alone. At least not in the year 2000. Very few people today would get up—in light of all you have just read and all the other semantic, superstitious, statistical, or religious "truths" we could offer about left-handedness—and declare that left-handed people are unfit to be parents, teachers, doctors, engineers, soldiers, or anything else on the basis of the inherent trait of handedness. But, in fact, until the early twentieth century, people were discriminated against in just these ways, beaten, and in some cases put to death simply for being left-handed. Being left-handed was considered without exception to be evil, a matter of choice, and a weakness that the individual could overcome.

However, over time, it is discrimination against left-handed people that has been overcome by rational scientific examination of nature, by logic, by awareness, by growing familiarity, and by reason—these last two, thankfully, most of all. It is our position that discrimination based on sexual orientation can be, will be, and is being similarly defeated. And, in this book, we hope to show that, for reasons of increased organizational productivity and profitability, it is in the absolute best interest of all workplaces to work to end discrimination based on sexual orientation.

WHAT THIS BOOK IS ALL ABOUT

In the preceding paragraphs, a few gauntlets were laid down that bear examination now. They concern language (use or nonuse of the word "lesbian"), the role of religion, and the cause of sexual orientation. These are examined in this chapter because they form the foundation for all that follows.

The remaining chapters concern themselves with the following:

- The business case for full inclusion of sexual orientation in diversity initiatives
- Mythology versus fact, laws, policies, and public opinion on a range of business and social issues that concern sexual orientation in the workplace
- Specific strategies for dealing proactively and reactively with full inclusion of sexual orientation
- An in-depth examination of workplace sexual orientation education programs
- A presentation of all the salient facts related to domestic partner benefits (DPBs)
- An analysis of the effect that the possible legalization of same-sex marriage could have on organizations of all kinds (primarily) in the United States
- The most frequently asked questions about sexual orientation in the workplace that cover a range of issues, concerns, and challenges
- A list of resources, references, and so forth for additional information or research

FOUNDATION ISSUES:
LANGUAGE, RELIGION AND TOLERANCE,
AND SCIENCE

In explaining the repeated use of the word *predominantly* earlier in this chapter, we said that little is absolute about the human animal. When we wrote the first edition of this book, we were very sure about a lot of things. As we write this second edition, we are less sure about some things because we have learned more about all things. We believe this fact will make this second book even better than the first.

Please don't misunderstand; we are not equivocating on anything that we believe. Most important, we do not equivocate one iota on our belief that sexual orientation is an inherent characteristic of a given individual. What we've learned in the last seven years has not shaken that basic belief a bit; we've learned that it is not "homosexuality" that is misunderstood so much as "sexual orientation."

This is a very important distinction because it seems that people are not able to accept the inherence of a nonheterosexual orientation due to the fact that they don't appreciate the inherence of a heterosexual orientation. They think only that to be nonheterosexual is a "choice" and to be heterosexual is "right." What they neglect to examine, what we hope people will examine more, is that neither is a choice and neither is right. Both just are. And like handedness, skin color, and head shape before it, orientation is assigned much too much importance (mostly) by people who don't understand it a bit.

So it is necessary to lay down the foundational elements of language, religion and tolerance, and science related to sexual orientation in order that people who pick up this book and read it understand the basis upon which it was written. You may disagree with the precepts, but unless you know what they are you will not be able to fully understand the strategies, programs, and initiatives that we advocate and explain.

Language

We don't subscribe to the use of the words *homosexual* (unless specifically being used in a clinical reference), *lesbian, queer, dyke,* or *faggot* to describe this part of ourselves because we feel no affinity to any of these terms.

The word *homosexual* was first used by Karl Maria Kertbeny in 1869 in Prussia when arguing for the repeal of that country's anti-homosexual laws. Another term used in the late nineteenth century and around the turn of the twentieth century was *sexual inversion* or, when describing a person, a *sexual invert.* This implies one who turns upside down or is opposite the standard position of a thing.

Homo, meaning "same," is an accurate enough word to use in describing a person's orientation and what it portends, but *homosexual* itself is rather stilted and long, and carries substantial misunder standing already; not to mention the degree of oversimplification it lends to something that is not so simple. Besides, Elton John is the only one who seems to pronounce it with any degree of class, so we don't use it.

The word *lesbian* derives from the Greek island of Lesbos where, it is said, in the sixth century B.C. resided a "warrior princess" (think Xena without the special effects, we imagine) named Sappho whose job was to do the dirty work of the emperor of the time. In her off hours, Sappho ran a school for young women and wrote poetry. In our opinion, very bad poetry but poetry nonetheless, some of which concerned itself with love between women. So, from this, we get *lesbian*, because they lived on Lesbos.

The word therefore has a legitimate etymology, but we find it stifling. First of all, we are not Greek and we truly despise Sappho's poetry (perhaps, in Liz's case, because she was forced to read a lot of it in a college fine arts class). Second, the implication is that by labeling one a "lesbian," her attractions, intimacies, friendships, what have you, are exclusively with other women. This is limiting beyond belief and contributes to the myth of the "man-hating lesbian."

Third, the word has been adopted by some nonheterosexual women (emphasis on "some") to purposefully create a separateness between themselves and (1) other women who are not nonheterosexual, (2) men, regardless of sexual orientation, and (3) anyone who doesn't view sexual orientation as a political issue.

We don't use this word because we fit in none of these categories. For the same reason, we don't subscribe to the use of the word *queer*, which strikes us as a very negative and argumentative term that also seems to be a rallying cry for separateness and the politicizing of sexual orientation.

We have no desire for separateness, to isolate ourselves from the male of the species in any way, or to politicize our sexual orientation even though others, as we'll see when we get to the discussion of equal rights in the workplace and in society, do.

People on both sides of the language question are vehement about the words used to describe them, and we are asked in our sessions all the time about the right word to use and are also called to task when we don't use "the right word." On many occasions at speaking opportunities and classes given by us in the last few years we have been told that we didn't speak for a given participant because we were not "queer" enough. That is true because we don't consider ourselves "queer" at all.

The answer is, there is no "right word to use," because people can—and do—make an argument for their own choices. However, in our opinion, some words are very definitely wrong to use when describing a person by sexual orientation. Two that come to mind are *dyke* and *fag*. True, some women and men have adopted these terms and use them freely as self-identifiers, sources of pride, signals of community, or even affectionately among friends. But for the most part, we have not matured or progressed enough as a society to be able to use these mostly derogatory terms peacefully, so we don't recommend that others do outside a knowing community or small circle of friends. They say World War I was started over less.

For the sake of this book, we use the word *gay* to describe issues related to sexual orientation in the workplace. Why *gay?* It actually comes down to, why not?

We find the word friendly and comfortable. It's not a tongue twister, doesn't require a foreign accent to make it palatable, and most people can spell it. Perhaps best of all, it doesn't denote exclusively women or exclusively men in any way and it doesn't limit those who are labeled to a single set of life-motivating factors. Plus, no one knows how its use started, so there are no preconceptions or cultural/political norms to overcome. The perfect word . . . with apologies to those who still feel it necessary to hum when they get to the part of the Christmas carol that refers to "our gay apparel." Perhaps nothing's perfect.

The use of the word *gay* is said to predate Kertbeny's coining of *homosexual*, but no one seems able to document that. There is evidence of its use, primarily in the gay subculture, as far back as the 1920s in both European and American cities. More than that is not evident.

Gay, therefore, is to nonheterosexual what *straight* is to heterosexual for the purposes of this book. Both friendly, inclusive, and hopefully noninsulting words. This work concerns itself only with the meaning of a person's nonheterosexual orientation in the workplace. That's all we intend to address.

As a last note about language, we don't mean to imply that transgendered people are being lumped together in this whole discussion because to be transgendered has nothing to do with sexual orientation. There is, however, a huge misconception about transgenderism, and transgendered people are typically associated with gay people in a big bag that these days is labeled "sexual minorities." This is a very inaccurate term that sheds no light on workplace issues related either to sexual orientation or to gender identification. Transgenderism, however, is an accurate term (albeit perhaps more misunderstood than even sexual orientation) and shedding some light on it won't do anyone any harm. Therefore, it does come up later in the book in the context of its importance to individuals at work.

Religion and Tolerance

According to polls published by the Human Rights Campaign (HRC), 64 percent of Americans believe that society has become more tolerant to sexual orientation. And, according to this survey, an even larger percentage believe that increased tolerance is desirable.

Tolerance is a difficult concept to assimilate when applied to inclusion if one considers only the part of its definition referring to "putting up with" or "enduring." But there is a part of tolerance that is all about the "capacity or practice of recognizing and respecting the opinions, practices, or behavior of others," and it is this expanded definition that we subscribe to when tolerance is applied to sexual orientation in the workplace.

A story in *USA Weekend* described a class called Promoting Tolerance Through Understanding that is taught in an Orange County, California, high school by a Joe Moros, who is by training and profession an English teacher.[2] Moros describes his class as "not English . . . not psychology . . . not social science. It's just what it is, a class in prejudice. It's a class in discrimination, hatred and violence."

The class explores these topics to get at the roots of them, disassemble them, dissolve them. He started teaching it in response to gang wars that were eating away at America's inner cities. He continues to teach it because it has had a documented positive effect on the social climate of his high school and community. He continues to teach it because it is fully subscribed each time it is offered. People come to learn, to debate, to argue . . . whatever. But they come.

Why do they come to a course devoted to the darker side of human nature? Because there is no place else to go.

When the New York Business Group on Health was first formed to create a class on HIV/AIDS for adults in America's workplaces, they did a very smart thing. They surveyed adults in the workplace and asked what kinds of courses these people wanted. They did not limit the subject to AIDS or STDs.

The response that they got back proved overwhelmingly that adults value workplace education more than any other source of information and that they wanted courses on HIV and AIDS, other STDs, on sexual orientation, people with disabilities, workplace violence, and a whole slew of other topics that we shy away from. Why did they want them? Precisely because we shy away from them.

It was found that adults feel that if employers take the time and spend the money to offer a course on a difficult, perhaps controversial, and potentially divisive topic such as orientation, then they do it because it is a worthwhile endeavor. If it wasn't, the time and money would not be allocated. Also, adults felt that it was exactly these topics that needed airing and discussion at work because these were real areas of potential conflict and discomfort for people. Americans, it turns out, don't immediately seek the easy way out. They seem to prefer identifying a challenge and overcoming it. This is the first reason why we are proponents of workplace education that engenders tolerance on the subject of sexual orientation of adults in the workplace.

The second reason we advocate inclusive education was better expressed by Judy Shepard (mother of murder victim Matthew Shepard) than we ever could. She said, as quoted in the *Denver Post,* "I feel very conflicted about Matthew becoming the gay-bashing poster boy. There's a climate in this country that sort of makes it OK to be homophobic. That's what scares parents, because nobody says 'Don't do that; that's not right.' "[3]

We believe that it is only through education that people find the courage and the information that fuels that courage to stand up and say, "Don't do that; that's not right."

Behavior, Not Beliefs

But what about the legitimate objections of those who oppose recognition of same-sex relationships on the basis of religion or morality?

Certainly it is no more right for nonheterosexual people or an organization to force a position down the throats of those who disagree than it is to allow any kind of workplace discrimination. What is the answer to this quandary? It's actually very simple: *In the workplace, it is behavior, not beliefs, that must guide all our actions.*

None of us checks our orientation at the door any more than we check our convictions there. But we all enter into a common agreement about *behavior at work* in support of common goals, usually productivity and/or profitability. There will be varying opinions about orientation as about other topics, but when those opinions lead to argument or to discrimination, the organization can and must step in to make certain demands on the behaviors of its workers.

An example we sometimes use in our class to demonstrate how religious beliefs can live respectfully in concert with workplace mandates has to do with the question of abortion. Although neither abortion nor sexual orientation necessarily should be issues with political, religious, moral, sexual, and social implications, they both currently are. Abortion polarizes people, upsets many, disrupts lives, influences legislation, and causes conflict sometimes to the point of violence. In short, its effects on some people are similar to those of sexual orientation.

Let's say that a given employee is "pro-life" on the abortion question—an oversimplification of a complicated position. But for the sake of this example, at work, all she does during free, nonwork time is harangue her fellow co-workers about abortion, about their need to protest it, about their need to sign petitions to outlaw it, about their need to pray about it, and so forth.

Take a minute to put yourself in the place of her supervisor. Assume, again for the sake of the example, that your position is also, generally speaking, pro-life. But consider the effect that this constant harping, handing out of pamphlets, and urging to march are having on your team's cohesiveness. Take a minute to consider the effect it is having not only on other pro-life members of your team, but also on "pro-choice" members.

Faced with this predicament, what do you think you'd do? When we've presented this example to managers, supervisors, or what have you in organizations throughout America for the last four or five years, the response has been, almost without fail, that they would take that person aside and quietly, respectfully, and likely without divulging their own position on the subject, tell her to cool it, immediately, or risk disciplinary action for destroying a safe, productive, and profitable work environment for everyone.

The point is that orientation must simply be accorded this same level of validity and respect . . . on both sides of the issue. People's opinions at work can live in balance with their professional responsibilities to the organization and to everyone in it. *A person's convictions, whatever their basis, can never be allowed to interfere with the principles of creating a positive work environment for all.* And if people, regardless of their position at a company, cannot set aside some convictions and do their job and allow others to do theirs, then they are entitled to get some information to help them bring their convictions in line with their responsibilities, typically in the form of information or education. Or they are entitled to leave and go elsewhere where they believe the values of the organization are more in line with their own.

There have been instances, no doubt, where people have left an organization because it started a nondiscrimination policy that included orientation, or because the organization implemented domestic partner benefits. This happens rarely, but it happens. And those people are to be respected for putting their livelihoods where their convictions are; but so should the organizations be respected for not letting a particular view result in discriminatory practices.

We must remember too that not all people, even of a shared denomination, feel the same about any issue that is potentially addressed in doctrine. As an example, a report was co-authored by religious leaders and the Human Rights Campaign called *Mixed Blessings.* It details the positions on sexual orientation of the nine largest Christian denominations and the four movements of Judaism in the United States. What's most striking about the report is that there is little agreement on so many of the issues related to sexual orientation not only among these schools of thought, but within them.[4]

The National Conference of Catholic Bishops issued a Pastoral Report called "Always Our Children—A Pastoral Message to Parents of Homosexual Children and Suggestions for Pastoral Ministers."[5] Among other things, this report asserted that:

- sexual orientation is an innate instinct;
- people should never reject their children on the basis of their orientation; and
- God does not love anyone less because of their sexual orientation.

While not everything related to orientation was either addressed or resolved in this paper, there is no doubt that it represents a major breakthrough in the Catholic Church's attitude on this subject.

In *Mixed Blessings,* the Human Rights Campaign reported that one of every three people who identify themselves as Christian believe that people should not be denied discrimination protection or equitable benefits on the basis of orientation.

It is possible, in short, to believe what you will about orientation and to, if we may borrow the phrase, "do unto others as you would have done unto you" by simply focusing on the stated expectations of behavior at work that are typically laid out in a nondiscrimination statement or code of conduct. And this is what all organizations must do. Leaders of businesses, universities, for-profit and nonprofit organizations and government entities must stop trying to hide behind some bizarre curtain of "morality" where sexual orientation is concerned. Gays are no longer the easy target they once were, not only because they are standing up and fighting back, but because so many other people are learning and thinking and acting upon this new knowledge in support of greater tolerance and inclusivity. The so-called "religious argument" has no more bearing on homosexuality than it does on anything else. It is much too complex a topic to generalize and discriminate against an entire classification of people based on one's "religion."

Kim Cromwell, senior consultant of diversity and change for Bank of Boston (now Fleet Boston Corporation), explained it this way: "If a group forms to discuss their religious convictions at work, that's okay. But if they form to oppress the beliefs of another group, then that is not appropriate in the workplace. We can't mandate acceptance, but we can have expectations about behavior at work because we have a responsibility as an employer to create an atmosphere where everyone feels safe."

This book presents strategies that allow organizations to deal with this area of conflict responsibly and respectfully, and very much in line with "behavior, not beliefs."

Science

The last foundation issue has to do with the authors' belief, call it insistence if you wish, that sexual orientation is an absolutely inherent characteristic in the human race and in the individual.

One could begin by asking, "Who cares?" and, in all honesty, that question occurs to us quite regularly too. As we'll discuss in a section of the book devoted to coming out (being truthful about something, in this case, your sexual orientation), when people fully incorporate their sexual orientation into their lives, it takes on a meaning that can only be described as trivial. If we were to ask 100 heterosexual people what they thought about being heterosexual, more than ninety-five would tell us that they give it little or no thought at all. We know this because we've done it.

On the flip side, ask 100 fully incorporated gay people what they think of their sexual orientation and they too will say that they don't think about it much. Again, we know this because we've done it.

But the truth is, for better or for worse, people do care about the origins of sexual orientation and it does seem to matter to some whether a person's orientation is determined by nature or nurture or choice. In declaring, with no doubt at all, that we believe orientations such as race, handedness, eye color, skin color, hair composition, and so forth to be absolutely hardwired in the genetic makeup of a given individual, we have faced two things that are also very certain. First, nothing about humanity or nature is that simple; and second, that if there is a genetic predisposition of human sexual orientation, then some extremely disturbed people will try to find it so that they can eradicate nonheterosexual orientation as if it were a disease.

With these two caveats in mind, a brief look at the evidence is warranted. Science has been looking for a "gay gene" longer than it has looked for a handedness gene (to carry through the analogy with which we started). In fact, science is not looking for a handedness gene and never has.[6] Perhaps this is because by the time it was possible to look for a genetic reason for handedness, people were over their bigotry against lefties.

The most famous study, still, having to do with sexual orientation was done by Alfred Kinsey and presented in two reports: *Sexual Behavior in the Human Male* (1948)[7] and *Sexual Behavior in the Human Female* (1953).[8] Whereas many people claim that Kinsey said that 10 percent of people are homosexual (or words to that effect), he said no such thing. Rather, Kinsey created a scale of human sexual response from 0 to 6, 0 denoting exclusive heterosexuality and 6 denoting exclusive homosexuality. Just the fact that he created a scale should tell us all something.

Kinsey believed that human sexual orientation, a term he didn't have at his disposal at the time, was determined by three things: predisposition to a certain sexual trigger, behavior, and thoughts/ fantasies. Based on these three factors and surveys of first 6,000 men and then 6,000 women for his reports, Kinsey concluded many things. One was that upward of 37 percent of the male population had had a homosexual experience after adolescence, that 13 percent had been primarily homosexual since then, and that 4 percent had been exclusively homosexual since then. For women, 13 percent had had a homosexual experience, 7 to 10 percent had been primarily homosexual since then, and 2 percent were exclusively homosexual. How this all generalizes to 10 percent is beyond us.

Since Kinsey's study, the percentages reported for homosexuality in the human animal have been as low as 2 percent and as high as 15 percent. Studies that also attempt to include bisexuality have shown results as high as 20 percent of humanity. Obviously, no one has found a way to answer this question to anyone's satisfaction. But our question is, even if it were only 1 percent of all humanity since the beginning of time, what would it matter? Does might make right? Do sheer numbers decide what is equitable, just, moral? We don't think so.

Back to science. Dean Hamer and Simon LeVay are scientists who have done research on the genetic predisposition to sexual orientation—that is, whether you will experience a sexual response in reaction to stimulus from a person of your own sex, the opposite sex, or to either sex. A study of female twins in 1993 found that almost 50 percent of identical twin sisters of gay women were gay themselves. Another study, released in July 1993, reported a link of male homosexuality to an area on the X chromosome. Hamer also released data in July 1993 that found more than 75 percent of a group of pairs of gay brothers had inherited identical DNA markers on a particular region of the X chromosome, which indicates a hereditary predisposition.[9]

None of this constitutes finding a "gay gene," but it remains unclear whether or not such evidence is warranted, necessary, or even remotely useful. There is no finding currently of a handedness gene or of a gene for eye color, intelligence, cancer, height, baldness, athletic ability, skin tone, muscle mass, resistance or susceptibility to virus, Tay-Sachs disease, or many other things. Yet these we accept as being inherent and attribute them in part to heredity (baldness, height, susceptibility) and in part to practicing and building upon whatever one is equipped with (athletic ability, intelligence).

What if sexual orientation is no more, or less, than any of this? An inherent predisposition in an individual. One that we all get; one that we all do with as we choose . . . but not one that we choose.

Ask yourself this. Can a left-handed person *be* right-handed? We think the answer is no. He can *do* things with his right hand if he chooses to, but he will not do them as well as he would do them with his left, and certainly the very act of trying, even if he perfected the skills, would be abnormal for him. We are both left-handed and both can write, if coerced, with our right hands. The problem is, no one can read what we've written with our right hands and the very act of doing so is uncomfortable and unnatural for us.

So, we can *act* right-handed, but we can't *be* right-handed. We are gay but we could act straight (and both did) but we never were straight. If you are straight, could you act gay? Do you think you could indulge a few stereotypes, dress differently, walk differently, hang out in different places than you typically do, engage in a sexual act foreign to you? You could indeed, but chances are you would find the whole experience unnatural and more than a little uncomfortable.

Another question. Why is the lack of hard evidence of a "gay gene" the thing that proves that being gay must be a choice? There is no evidence of an appendicitis gene or a left-handed gene or an intelligence gene. Does that make these things choices?

People also say that to be nonheterosexual is unnatural and abnormal. Look at the latter first. *Normal* is defined as "conforming to a usual or typical standard." The definition inconveniently leaves out what (or who) determines what is usual or typical. Again, there is no argument, even from us, that roughly 80 percent of all people are heterosexual. But we would argue that no standard has been set that could reasonably suggest that 20 percent is the line at which things are not normal.

Unnatural is much more interesting to dissect because *natural* is defined as "present in or produced by nature." *Nature* is defined as "the order, disposition, and essence of all entities composing the physical universe." So, if nonheterosexuality were unnatural, it would not exist in nature, but nothing could be further from the truth.

According to Bruce Bagemihl in *Biological Exuberance* there is evidence of homosexuality in more than 450 species.[10] There is no reason to doubt that if his studies ever go beyond these 450, the findings would be the same.

In an interview with Deb Price in the *Detroit News* after his book's publication, Bagemihl reported that male-female pairing beyond momentary encounters is found in only 5 percent of mammals, and the most successful families in species such as the red-billed black swan and the grizzly bear are same-sex father (swan) or mother (bear) families. He also reported that 90 percent of California's northern elephant seal males never attempt to breed.

Other findings showed that pairs of male walruses spoon while sleeping; that gay female rhesus monkeys flirt, kiss, and engage in courtship games found only among them; and that male giraffes sensually neck only with one another.

Although this doesn't prove that nonheterosexuality is inherent in the human animal, it certainly does dispel the myths that people are the only ones with a variety of sexual orientations, and orientations other than heterosexual ones are unnatural.

THE POINT IS THIS: EVERYONE CHOOSES

Ultimately, we base this entire book on the fact that sexual orientation is as inherent a characteristic as any other—the good ones and the bad ones—for which the proof of inherence is mostly anecdotal and widely accepted. People say that we can't prove that orientation is inherent; we say that our being here is proof enough. We never had to ask ourselves if we were gay any more than our straight siblings ever asked themselves if they were straight. This fact is not political to us. We *don't* mean it to suggest that because people are "born this way" they should not be discriminated against. We *do* mean that just because a person is a person, he or she should not be discriminated against.

In order for people to be the best they can be, to live and work up to their potential, they must be able to freely be who they are and use to the fullest extent possible the hand that they were dealt. This is the message of this book. This is most true in our workplaces because it is there that we are expected to put forth our best effort. If we are spending more time hiding our orientation from our co-workers than we are thinking about the tasks at hand, then we are shortchanging not only our employers and our teammates, we are also shortchanging ourselves.

We believe that who you are is who you are; what you do with who you are is the only thing that is entirely up to you. For example, we will not argue that there are not women in this world who were sexually abused in childhood by males and, as a response to that, have chosen to live as gay women in sexual or otherwise intimate relationships with other women. But this does not necessarily mean that their sexual orientation is homosexual; what it means is that they have made a choice about what they will do. It doesn't change who they are.

People say that gays make choices. That's true. All people make choices, but not about their sexual orientation. We choose, as individuals, to act in concert with our orientation, or we choose not to. For gay people, the actual choice is weighing economic survival and survival in general against hostility, humiliation, and fear. For straight people, the choice is whether to reexamine deeply ingrained beliefs. For employers, a big choice faced daily—now more than ever—is how they will treat all of their employees. Only one thing is certain in this triangle of choice: Personal beliefs must never be an issue in the workplace, only personal behavior. Or, to put it another way, the rights of every individual in the workplace to work in a safe environment must never depend on someone else's highly subjective beliefs or opinions.

Chapter 2

Sexual Orientation at Work: The Business Case

Diversity in the workplace is attracting so much attention because of economics. The composition of the talent pool and the existing workforce along with the market for products and services—regardless of whether you are in the public, private, or education market sector—is dominated by groups heretofore thought of strictly as minorities. These include but are not limited to women, people of color, Hispanic Americans, Asian Americans, gay people, and people with disabilities. People with disabilities alone can, and do, trigger policy changes, program enhancements, and opportunities for revenue growth on almost a daily basis; what it means to be "disabled" broadens continually, and so accommodations, opportunities must broaden right along with it.

Organizations are not working on diversity initiatives to make themselves seem "friendlier" to these emerging constituencies; they are working on these initiatives to enhance the competitive edge of the corporation through proactive development and integration of the strengths of these people.

Diversity management is viewed now more than ever as a business issue and less as strictly a human resources issue. The distinction is a crucial one. Although management does not doubt that proper management and support programs are important, those programs have not been hardwired to the bottom line. Some shadowy relationship between taking care of your people and their resulting performance has always been acknowledged, but it was never considered an empirical cause and effect. That is changing. Due to people such as Edward Hubbard, these changes are no longer just anecdotal; they can be proven with data.

In his book, Hubbard presents a workable model for giving a quantitative value to diversity efforts in the workplace.[1] His tools include over 100 formulas to report the effect that diversity initiatives have on bottom-line performance. He also provides ways of assessing the return on investment of such efforts, ways to track and monitor changes due to diversity initiatives, and ways to ensure that the initiatives are connected meaningfully to the business case for the programs. These tools may not be perfect, but neither they nor anything like them have been available before, and they are intensely necessary for businesses where numbers drive everything. And indeed, there may not be a business that exists, again regardless of sector, where numbers don't drive everything.

REAL DATA

Louise Young, cochair of the Human Rights Campaign Business Council, developed a simple formula to estimate the cost of an inequitable workplace.[2] Her formula assumes a 5 percent nonheterosexual population, which we consider too conservative. We will use what we believe is a more realistic—although also very conservative—10 percent. And she uses 10 percent as the amount of productivity lost in an unsafe and inequitable workplace.

Using her model with these percentages, a company employing 5,000 people will have 500 employees who are not heterosexual. If the average salary is $40,000 and the average loss of productivity per nonheterosexual worker is $4,000 ($40,000 × 10 percent = $4,000), then the annual loss to the company is estimated to be $2,000,000.

Take Microsoft, for example. It has publicly said that it believes *each* employee it loses to the competition or to less than optimum productivity is worth $2,000,000 over the estimated average duration of employment of a Microsoft employee. Using their own calculations, if they lost the productivity of 10 percent of their workforce due to a less than equitable workplace, their losses would skyrocket into billions of dollars. Given their annual revenue and scope of products, this is not an unreasonable estimate.

The first edition of *Straight Talk* reported that it's a matter of record that companies with progressive, people-oriented strategies experience better results in terms of customer satisfaction, profitability, and global competitiveness. The stocks of the companies listed in *The 100 Best Companies to Work for in America* did then—and still do—outperform Standard and Poor's 500 stock price over a ten-year average.

The book *The Change Masters* by Rosabeth Moss Kanter compared forty-seven companies, chosen by human resources professionals for their progressive policies, with firms of equal size in their industries.[3] The progressive companies were more profitable and enjoyed greater growth and return on investment over a twenty-year span than the comparison companies.

Progressiveness is reflected by a slight but palpable shift from a reactive ("let's avoid the negatives") to a proactive ("what can we do before the competition does?") mind-set. By finding ways to get ahead of a problem or a potential problem, companies can enhance their profitability. The potential benefits include gaining market share, improving their competitive advantage for labor and patronage, and taking full advantage of their greatest resource—all the people, gay and straight, who work for them.

Tracking the policies of organizations relative to their treatment of nonheterosexual employees is becoming extremely sophisticated. Organizations are listed in the resources section of this book whose sole mission is to do this kind of tracking and compare what they learn to the market performance of the organizations being scrutinized.

One of these, the *Gay and Lesbian Values Index*[4] (GLV Index) has been able to create a credit scale by which a value is assigned to organizational policies that do things such as:

- Evaluate the incorrect use of "sexual preference" as compared to "sexual orientation"
- Include mention of transgender personnel
- Publicly support nonprofit or political gay interest groups
- Lend a hand in the fight against breast cancer and HIV
- Offer diversity training inclusive of sexual orientation

These are just some of the criteria measured. By assigning credit points to an organization's performance on each, the organization can be both rated independently and ranked as compared to others. This information about the companies is made widely known to consumers of all sexual orientations who care about full inclusion for whatever reason.

What's happening with efforts such as those of the GLV Index is that hard numbers are being assigned in defensible ways to the policies of organizations that directly affect their human resources. These are sometimes called "soft" policies. Nothing is anecdotal and no allowance is made for vague ideas such as "It's better to work for us in New England than it is in the South" as used to be the case. Companies are being called to task using the one thing that matters most to them—money and the potential to make or lose it. It is no longer possible (and never was true anyway) to assume that it would be okay to treat gay people a certain way in the South but that such behavior would be unacceptable up North. America doesn't work that way. We do not discriminate by geography.

PROFITABILITY

If the point of your diversity management efforts is to create a harassment-free, satisfactory, cooperative, productive, and profitable workplace for all, then you must include sexual orientation as a diversity factor. Doing so pushes the envelope less than it did a mere five years ago, but it still bears significant baggage. Whereas in 1976 only one Fortune 500 company used inclusive nondiscrimination language, in 1999 there were 260.[5] In 1995, the federal government offered no protection to federal workers on the basis of sexual orientation, but as of 1998, federal workers (outside the military) are protected. Both of these things are very good, but neither constitutes 100 percent in their sectors and efforts won't be remotely satisfactory until it does constitute 100 percent.

The push toward 100 percent will accelerate as data regarding profitability of organizations with fully inclusive programs and policies becomes better known.

When your organization goes ahead and does something to positively acknowledge sexual orientation, can you expect to be penalized, in real time, in the marketplace? The answer is a resounding "no." More than that, it appears that discriminatory practices are the ones that hurt an organization moneywise and that progressiveness in this area actually, literally, pays.

Consider that after passing Proposition Two, prohibiting "special rights" for homosexuals, our home state of Colorado suffered a documented loss of convention and tourism revenues in excess of $120 million. The fact that Prop Two was later overturned never helped to recover a nickel of those funds, and more damaging is the fact that during the boycott, people discovered that skiing in Utah or Montana was very nice indeed and have never come back to Colorado.

Portland, Oregon, lost $15 million in convention revenue after an antigay initiative was put on a ballot, even though the initiative itself was defeated. Cobb County, Georgia, gave up an estimated $10 million in Olympic Games revenue when fair-minded people convinced the Olympic Committee to move the volleyball competition to another county because of Cobb's exclusionary practices. Coors Brewing Company, L.L. Bean, Cracker Barrel, Domino's Pizza, Allstate Insurance, Texaco, and ExxonMobil have all found themselves on the wrong side of consumer actions against discriminatory practices. Most changed their tunes when the revenue figures were released. Why? Because discrimination is bad business.

Part of the reason for this is that because we are talking about the specific requirements of people relative to their orientation, there are two things we can't forget. First, everyone has a sexual orientation, and so *everyone* is potentially affected by such discrimination. Second, all people have allies. In this case, all developing data from court cases to public opinion polls indicate that the tide is turning to a greater acceptance of nonheterosexual orientation, and that provisions must be made for these differences in people's lives.

A 1999 poll indicated that more than 90 percent of all Americans believe that gay people should have equal rights in terms of employment and public accommodations. This is up from just 56 percent in 1977, 71 percent in 1989, 85 percent in 1997, and 87 percent in 1998.

The proportion of Americans who believe that civil rights laws for gays and lesbians are intended to secure *equal rights* and not special rights is up to 54 percent from only 41 percent in 1995. And the number who believe that society is becoming more tolerant, generally speaking, is 64 percent. Well over 75 percent of us believe that increased tolerance is a good thing.[6]

When the Walt Disney Corporation implemented domestic partner benefits they were the subject of a large, organized boycott attempt by a particular religious organization. The boycott failed and the company posted better than expected profits and revenues compared to the previous year's same fiscal period. Since that time, other large and very public, symbolic organizations such as AT&T, United Airlines, American Airlines, US Airways, Shell Oil, Chevron, the Bank of America, General Mills, and literally hundreds of others have implemented these benefits without hearing a peep in protest from anyone. Americans do not boycott to promote discrimination; they boycott to stop it.

The gay market segment is, according to Mulryan/Nash and the Simmons Market Research Bureau, one of the fastest, if not the fastest, growing demographic for products and services in the United States.[7] Since 1997, the first year that revenues in gay-targeted media exceeded $100 million dollars, ad revenues have continued to grow in that market at a rate of more than 25 percent per year. And there are over 100 local newspapers and seven or more national gay-focused magazines in the United States at the turn of the twenty-first century. A scant five years ago, we counted twenty newspapers and two national magazines.

Does niche advertising contribute to revenue? Yes, it most certainly does. Research shows that the gay market is one of the most attention starved and loyal, and an easy area for marketers to build early dominance in if they take the plunge.[8] Be advised, though, that there is no truth to the nonsensical self-serving rhetoric that gay people are either economically or educationally privileged. But there is great truth in the idea that the gay market is open to organizations that take its requirements into consideration both as employees and patrons. All people vote with their wallets—this doesn't depend on how much their wallets hold.

Any conversation about profitability must also take into account internal factors, i.e., human resources. In an economy with literally thousands of jobs going begging, which is choking the potential growth of organizations of all sizes, companies cannot afford to be discriminatory. This is undoubtedly not just a human resources problem anymore.

People make significant investments in themselves; when they go out into the working world, they expect return on those investments. Any decisions by an employer of any type that are reflected overtly in published hiring policies or covertly in the initiatives of the company to provide only for a certain race, gender, or orientation will result in an enormous loss of competitive positioning for the company. As more organizations offer protection and equitable benefits, people working in less progressive companies get up and move to them.

Look at it this way. If any corporation tried to turn back the clock to the year 1940 or so and today told all its black employees that they were unwelcome to use the same toilets or eat in the same cafeteria as whites, that organization could reasonably expect trouble in the form of lowered morale, lessened productivity, and loss of profitability. Most, if not all, of its black employees would walk out the door. Or if any organization publicly stated that no woman working within it should expect to rise in the ranks higher than administrative assistant or assistant professor, it could not feign surprise if the women working there gave less than their all or left altogether. Either scenario would probably lead to public outrage and boycotting of the company's products. And this is exactly the kind of treatment being faced by workers on the basis of their sexual orientation. It is wasteful and very shortsighted.

Take the case of ExxonMobil, now the largest corporation in the world. As this is being written, Exxon, the dominant party in the merger, is removing language in Mobil's nondiscrimination policy referring to sexual orientation and is also reneging on Mobil's policy of providing workplace partner benefits to its employees. They are doing this because they say that their nondiscrimination policy is inclusive enough, and that it is not their place to decide what constitutes a valid relationship.

Since their decision was announced in the last month of the twentieth century, a groundswell of negativity has been directed at the company. Their own unions (who are unaffected by these decisions due to in-force collective bargaining agreements), *The New York Times, The Wall Street Journal,* the Hearst and Knight-Ridder newspapers, the Turner companies, and thousands of other organizations large and small have denounced the ExxonMobil position and action as being counterproductive, mean-spirited and, in this economic climate, downright stupid.

If a statement such as "we don't discriminate against anybody" were good enough, then there would be no need at all for Federal Equal Employment Opportunity (EEO) guidelines, civil rights laws, or the suspect classes being given their due in the Constitution. As for the corporation having to decide what constitutes a legal relationship, that is unnecessary. Legal relationships are already well defined by tax code and what constitutes a domestic partnership or valid relationship has been pretty well agreed upon and in practice since about 1982.

ExxonMobil is an employer that has not paid attention to history and so will now be forced to repeat it. The history is this: By breaking down barriers for women and minorities in the workplace, the lesson learned is that a policy of inclusion results in more creativity, greater productivity, and a larger applicant pool from which to draw qualified candidates. It is vital to eliminate barriers that keep people out of the workforce for reasons unrelated to their basic abilities, but in fact, that is exactly the opposite of what ExxonMobil has done and the damage will be close to irreversible for many years.

Many corporations, colleges and universities, and religious, political, civil, professional, and scientific groups already realize the importance of being gay-supportive. For businesses and corporations, a supportive stance results in becoming an employer of choice for many people—not just gay people, but for all concerned about a fair, equitable, and nonhostile work environment. Why should this be? There are two good reasons: the laws of the land we live in and the families from which we come.

THE LAW AND THE FAMILY

People confuse, we're afraid, laws about sexual orientation with laws about sodomy. Sexual orientation is a part of human sexuality, an inherent characteristic, and therefore a characteristic of us all. We all have one. Sodomy, on the other hand, is a behavior or set of behaviors that some people have, in the course of U.S. history, taken it upon themselves to outlaw.

Sodomy is outlawed in eighteen states (as of January 2000). In thirteen of those, heterosexual sodomy is just as illegal as homosexual sodomy, even within the bounds of marriage. What this means is that heterosexual married couples break the law with alarming regularity in the privacy of their own homes. Many people, when they look up sodomy and then research to see if what they are reading about is illegal in their state, feel quite insulted, as well they should. Such things are not the business of anyone to legislate, certainly not in a mature society. Signs of our growing maturity are evident in the fact that a short five years ago, sodomy was illegal in about a third more states than it is now. People are learning.

The point for our purposes here, though, is that homosexuality is not illegal. There are no illegal sexual orientations. Laws seek to legislate our behavior, not our orientation. This is an area of great misunderstanding that is easily and effectively corrected in an educational or otherwise informational program.

The legal landscape in relation to gay rights changes continually. As of this writing, the rights of individuals based on their sexual orientation are not protected by the U.S. Constitution. There is no federal job protection on the basis of sexual orientation. An act that would provide this protection, called the Employment Non-Discrimination Act (see Appendix E for details of what ENDA provides for) was introduced in 1994 and has yet to be passed into law by Congress—this in spite of overwhelming public support for its passage.

Nondiscrimination laws that apply to employment (and typically to housing, public accommodations, and credit as well) are in force in only eleven of the United States (as of October 2000) These are Hawaii, California, Nevada, Wisconsin, Minnesota, Vermont, Connecticut, New Jersey, Massachusetts, New Hampshire, and Rhode Island. Minnesota is the only of these to similarly protect the rights of its transgendered citizens.

There are about 180 to 200 cities or municipalities with ordinances that extend job protection to people on the basis of their orientation, but ordinances do not carry the weight of law. Additionally, eight states have executive orders barring discrimination in public employment on this basis: Colorado, Maryland, New Mexico, New York, Ohio, Pennsylvania, Iowa, and Washington. Two states, Illinois and Michigan, have civil service rules that prohibit discrimination.

If you operate in a state, city, county, or town that has a nondiscrimination law or order specifically inclusive of sexual orientation, but your company does not specifically include sexual orientation as a protected characteristic in its nondiscrimination codes, then the organization is in violation of local statutes and can be sued or brought before your state's human rights commission.

Organizations can expect more of their gay employees to insist upon discrimination protection and the resulting, or what should be resulting, equitable benefits in the workplace. And those organizations would do well to listen. The reason is simple. In those places where the law does not protect and provide for inclusion of sexual orientation minorities, gay people work under enormous strain. They cannot perform at their best under these oppressive circumstances. In many cases, discrimination may be unlawful; in all cases, it is unproductive and unprofitable.

The construct of the family is also a driving factor in the conversation about sexual orientation in the workplace. Employers are recognizing that the dynamics of "the family" are changing, and that these changes result in different economic and social requirements for their workforce. This has profound implications for the organization's family-based programs and policies.

The traditional family has long been defined as a wage earner husband/father, a homemaker wife/mother, and their two children under age eighteen, all living under one roof. This construct of the family has not applied to the majority in the United States since World War II. It has not existed among the poorer segments of our society for much longer than that because rarely did the wives/mothers in lower income families have the option of being homemakers.

Today, nontraditional family units far outnumber traditional ones. According to researchers at the University of Chicago at the end of 1999, the percentage of households made up of married couples with children dropped from 45 percent in the early 1970s to just 26 percent in 1998. They also found that:[9]

- 56 percent of adults were married as compared to 75 percent in 1972;
- 51 percent of children live at home with their two biological parents as opposed to 73 percent in 1972;
- the percentage of households made up of unmarried people with no children was double the 1972 rate (more than 33 percent, compared to 16 percent);
- 18.2 percent of children live with a single parent as compared to 4.7 percent in 1972; and
- only 67 percent of Americans believe that people should stay married "for the sake of their kids." And 1999 was the first year that question was ever asked.

What does all this mean? It means simply that the family is very multidimensional and that "family values" is not a term with only one meaning. In the 1997 Family Survey conducted by the U.S. Census Bureau, 1.4 million couples self-identified as gay-based families and the number of unmarried domestic partnerships, regardless of orientation of the parties, had increased 400 percent since the 1970s.[10]

For the first time, Canada's next census (scheduled for 2001) will ask people about their sexual orientation. According to Pierre Turcotte, Statistics Canada's chief of housing, family, and social statistics, "there's been nothing on sexual orientation" so far in census collection but, according to him, "we had a lot of people telling us that they wanted the information on this."[11]

In Canada, the federal justice and finance departments, the provinces, academic researchers, and insurance companies are among those who are interested in tracking this aspect of Canadian demographics. There is little reason to think that marketing organizations are not also intensely interested in getting this data; nor is there any reason to think that the same is not true in the United States.

The structure of the family is changing because the family is, and always has been, a dynamic unit. In a BBC program about the family it said, "the family must be learned, practiced, and rehearsed. It is not a force of nature; it is a work of art."

The workforce too is a work of art—a living, functioning, vital entity that each organization creates from the magnificent palette called the human race. The workforce comes from and is a reflection of the same forces shaping and reshaping the family. It is more than logical to conclude that if less than one-quarter of all family units are traditional in nature, then fewer than one-quarter of workers are bringing "traditional family values" to the workplace. But they are most certainly bringing family values and requirements to work, along with the requirement to be acknowledged, accommodated, and incorporated at work and in society.

Nontraditional families come in a variety too diverse and flavorful to list here . . . if only because we would most certainly leave someone's family out. These families function the same way as traditional families do, but some people refuse to acknowledge that. It's vital to the success of all organizations that this be acknowledged because "the family" continues to serve as the foundation for many human resources policies and workplace benefits and programs. If the yardstick by which the family is measured is no longer valid, then the possibility exists that far too many employees are not being treated or compensated equitably.

THE BUSINESS CASE IN WORDS

The business case for full inclusivity is still expressed in words as well as numbers. At the Deluxe Corporation, a Fortune 700 company and the largest financial printer in the world, management laid down the following challenges for the organization:

- If we meet the needs of an increasingly diverse customer marketplace because we are constantly researching untapped markets in the United States and they are primarily composed of people of color, people with disabilities, people over forty-five years old, among others, and
- If we understand the new skilled workers because in the United States, by the year 2005, the net new entrants into the workforce will be 85 percent minorities, women, and immigrants, and
- If we incorporate diversity in our globalization efforts because we are looking at regions well beyond our North American borders, and
- If we better use our workforce because underutilization of the workforce is related to a loss in productivity and ultimately to our bottom-line earnings, then we will succeed in:

  —Fully using the talents and experiences of our associates to maximize our productivity in meeting the challenges of the increasingly diverse marketplace
  —Providing continuous quality improvement through understanding our new skilled workers and effectively exchanging knowledge with our current and new business partners
  —Being a global leader in providing the best services and products to our customers
  —Being the employer of choice for our associates
  —Being the model of the best business practices in our industries
  —Gaining an abundance of competitive advantages

Shell Exploration and Production Company (SEPCo), an affiliate of Shell Oil Company, has developed a document, *Diversity Performance Standard,* whose purpose is to be a roadmap for creating an environment of inclusion within the company.[12]

This document has two focal points. The first is a matrix that Shell's SEPCo has created to diagram "a performance standard and assessment tool to help achieve an environment of inclusion where Diversity excellence promotes business success." The matrix comprises the steps that business units can and should take to measure their performance in, and relative to, diversity management in the SEPCo workplaces.

These steps fall into the categories of leadership and commitment; employee engagement; work relationships; opportunities and fairness; demographics; family and personal life balance; and community. The stages that each business unit is encouraged to pass through for each category are (in order): awareness of, understanding of, acceptance of, and commitment to diversity in each.

What's remarkable about the document, beyond being a state-of-the-art examination of the practical business aspects of workplace diversity, is the obvious amount of time, energy, and resources that went into it. Anyone fortunate enough to analyze it comes away with a much deeper understanding of how diversity impacts the bottom line of an organization for everyone, regardless of job title, function, or place in the hierarchy.

Why does an organization such as Shell Exploration and Production put so many people, so much time, and so much money into this task?

> One reason that valuing Diversity is so important to our business is that the *only way* to truly succeed is to fully utilize the talents of every person in our company. That is how we can achieve both our collective and individual potential. To do otherwise is not acceptable at a time when we need all hands on deck. Without the sense of belonging, respect and value that all individuals require, we risk losing our most valuable assets . . . the talents of our people and our reputation in the community.[13] [italics in original]

Makes us wish that Shell, instead of Exxon, had bought Mobil.

NONDISCRIMINATION AND PUBLIC OPINION

This brings us to the role of nondiscrimination policies and practices and how they play in America. In our work as sexual orientation educators, we've been informed more than once before going somewhere that we could expect less than a gracious welcome. Negative things have been said to us when we've traveled south of the Mason-Dixon Line, for sure, but they have also been said to us when traveling to locations on the Pacific Ocean, just south of the Canadian border, and just north of the Rio Grande.

We have also been told that we can get away with what we do (education programs inclusive of orientation and/or the implementation of domestic partner benefits), in white-collar businesses or among the white-collar parts of production businesses, but we can't be successful in blue-collar industries or among blue-collar workers. What we've learned perhaps better than anything else in the last seven years is that it is ridiculous and wasteful to assume that people hold a bias against us due to where they live, what they do for a living, or how far they went in school.

Here are the facts. Seventy percent of Americans support the right of nonheterosexuals to serve in the military. More than half of all Republicans, more than two-thirds of Independents, and more than three-quarters of Democrats back antidiscrimination laws inclusive of sexual orientation. All of these statistics represent a one-third increase since 1992.[14]

A majority of Americans support both the Employment Non-Discrimination Act and the Hate Crimes Prevention Act. A majority of Americans support certain rights and benefits for gay partners, including hospital visitation rights, inheritance rights, and workplace health care benefits. And the majority of Americans don't understand that gay Americans don't share these rights at the start of the twenty-first century.

In Chapter 1 we wrote that the two primary driving factors increasing tolerance of sexual orientation in the United States were growing familiarity and people making reasoned decisions. The statistics bear this out.

In 1983, only 23 percent of Americans reported having a gay friend. In 1994, only 43 percent reported having a gay friend. In 1998,

55 percent of Americans said they have a gay friend or acquaintance. Coincident with all this familiarity, people are more reasonable about the validity of same-sex relationships, with approval of them, according to Gallup, leaping to 54 percent from well under 35 percent in less than eight years. The people at the National Opinion Research Center tracked an increase in approval of same-sex relationships during the same period as going from 58 percent to 73 percent.[15]

What does this mean to business? It means that when an organization is fully inclusive, it is also fully in step with the majority of its employees, patrons, clients, customers, and other stakeholders. And yet we must acknowledge that some are hesitant or want to avoid the subject altogether . . . and some, such as ExxonMobil, take giant leaps backward.

They fear that they will lose market share if they take a progressive stance in policies of workplace inclusion, specifically in relation to gay people, when, as the statistics prove, exactly the opposite is true. They are afraid that having an inclusive policy will be interpreted as giving tacit approval to something and that customers who hold the opposite view will withdraw their business. The Disney episode proves that the latter is simply not true and, again, the statistics prove that the former is no longer true either.

John M. Conley and William M. O'Barr, anthropologists at Duke University, responded to a hypothetical situation presented in the *Harvard Business Review*.[16] In this scenario, a valued employee of a financial services company notifies his boss that he intends to bring his same-sex partner to an upcoming corporate function at which clients will be present. The boss worries that in making his sexual orientation known, the employee may put some client relationships in jeopardy.

Conley and O'Barr maintain that it is neither economically necessary nor morally justifiable for organizations, even conservative ones, to "conform to the meaner aspects of their clients' cultures." For a long time, they point out, elite law firms insisted that the exclusion of women and racial minorities was justifiable because their clients just wouldn't stand for female or black lawyers. But, in fact, firms did start to diversify and the clients did stand for it.

An organization should not, according to these anthropologists, make the mistake of underestimating its customers. If institutions use their predictions of another's response as an excuse to not do what they know is right and is good business, they are missing the boat on their enormous opportunity to exercise the influence that can shape a culture and grab more market share. "We believe," they wrote, "that the history of elite law firms and others suggests that, in the long run, the moral choice is the lucrative one as well. When major changes in cultural values take place, *it pays* to be ahead of the trend rather than running behind making excuses."

Chapter 3

Myths and Facts:
Sexual Orientation
in Business and Society

Discrimination against people because of sexual orientation is wasteful in every sense. To counteract this discrimination, we must first understand it. To fully understand it, we must face head-on the condition called homophobia and its pervasiveness as an excuse against progressive and equitable workplace policies for gay people.

Homophobia is a term as misused and misunderstood as any other you could think of. We will explain it here as a stand-alone item and also in terms of the effect its—mostly unproductive—visibility has in politics, in religion, and in our families. Finally, we will look at its effects in the workplace by disassembling mythology about gay people.

HOMOPHOBIA

If translated literally, the word means "fear of sameness." Semantics can be delightfully ironic. It is the fact that gays are the same as heterosexuals, save their physical and/or emotional attractions, that most confounds. And it is the overemphasis on physical and/or emotional attractions that makes all the arguing about sexual orientation so patently ridiculous. As gay women we are constantly amazed at how much stock people who object to us put in that part of our lives; they give it much more credence than we do and assign it much more importance in our lives than in their own. There's something very sad about that, and, of course, also ironic when you consider that gay people are the ones who are supposed to be ruled by sexual activity. The truth is, we don't bring it up nearly as often as people who haven't a clue about us do.

The more typical definition of homophobia is "the irrational fear and hatred of homosexuals" which is pretty accurate in describing how the condition plays itself out. It is irrational in every sense; once reason is applied and understanding is gained about sexual orientation, fear and hatred typically disappear.

Homophobia is not just destructive to gay people. It hurts everyone:

- It inhibits the ability of straight people to form close relationships with people of their own sex, for fear of being labeled gay.
- It locks people into rigid gender roles that squelch creativity and self-expression.
- It compromises human integrity by pressuring people to treat others badly and frequently contrary to their basic humanity.
- Combined with HIV-phobia, it results in the lack of forthright sex education in business and in schools, the lack of which contributes heavily to the continued spread of HIV and other STDs.
- It prevents some gay people from developing an authentic self-identity and adds to the pressure to conform to a heterosexual standard which, in the long run, is destructive not only to them but to their spouses, children and other family members.
- It inhibits appreciation for all human diversity by limiting acceptance of those who are outside of the mainstream as defined, typically in grossly limited ways, by the individual.[1]

Homophobia, according to the Campaign to End Homophobia, comes in four types: personal, interpersonal, institutional, and cultural.[2] By combining these types with the three biases that, according to Gregory Herek of the University of California, cause homophobia, it is possible to get a very detailed and much more correct idea of what homophobia really is. The biases identified by Herek are: experiential, defensive, and symbolic.[3]

Personal Homophobia

An individual's belief that gay people are sick, immoral, inferior to straight people, or incomplete as men or women is called *personal homophobia*. People who are personally homophobic are not always straight. Many gay people are intensely homophobic. This phenomenon is called *internalized homophobia* and it occurs in gay people who have been battered by their families or society for so long that they come to believe that they really are somehow deficient. People who suffer from internalized homophobia are the people in the workplace who remain closeted voluntarily; not because they fear what others will say, but because of their own misunderstanding and discomfort with themselves. It is a very unhealthy situation.

Personal homophobia is caused by what Herek calls a "defensive bias." When people believe that the image they project does not match that of a "real man" or a "real woman" (whatever those terms mean to that individual), and that they might be labeled gay because of it, this makes them defensive and leads to what is typically called personally homophobic behavior.

Interpersonal Homophobia

The fear, dislike, or hatred of people believed to be gay is called *interpersonal homophobia*. It is likely to show itself in the form of name-calling, verbal and physical harassment, or widespread acts of discrimination. Violent harassment of gays, also called gay bashing, all too frequently results in death.

Homophobia, generally speaking, has long been considered "the last acceptable prejudice." Everyone knows that gays are sick or evil or both, so bashing them is not so bad. There is no such thing as an acceptable prejudice, especially when that prejudice results in physical pain or injury. The aspect of interpersonal homophobia that is most disturbing is that it is usually taught. But that means it can be untaught.

It is important to point out that most people act out their interpersonal homophobia in ways that are not physically violent. But the violence they perpetrate on gay family members, friends, or co-workers is no less devastating. Relatives who shun or vilify their gay parents, children, siblings, or other relatives; a military that casts aspersions on a person's desire and ability to serve his or her country; and a work place that does not acknowledge the requirements of those with a nonmajority orientation all wreak devastating emotional cruelty on those affected.

Herek believes that one cause of interpersonal homophobia—whether expressed with physical or mental violence—is an experiential bias. This arises when a person who has had a bad experience with any type of person (or animal or thing) projects that experience to all people of the same type.

In other words, if a woman is approached by a gay female friend or acquaintance in a way that makes her feel uncomfortable, she may assume from that point on that all gay women will try to approach her that way. To understand how illogical this reaction is, she has only to think of her experience with men. In all likelihood she has at some point spurned the inappropriate advances of a male without concluding that all men will approach her in similarly inappropriate ways.

Interpersonal homophobia rooted in experiential bias is at the crux of the whole "don't ask, don't tell" debate regarding gays in the military. At the dawn of the twenty-first century, one of the principal architects of that archaic and hypocritical policy admitted that it all came down to how one soldier would feel about having to share a space blanket for body warmth with another soldier if the former knew that the latter were gay.[4] The immaturity and stupidity of this boggles the mind and we can only wonder if this man, in his fifties and a retired very high-ranking officer, realizes how ridiculous he sounded repeating it as justification for the policy.

The second possible cause for interpersonal homophobia, according to Herek, is a symbolic bias that is driven by the belief that homosexuality destroys closely held value systems. Our values and belief systems help each of us get through this life, and we can react badly to whatever we feel threatens them. Symbolic biases drive some organizational efforts, hiding under cloaks of heightened morality, to attempt to scapegoat all gay people for the ills in the world. These organizations would be better served, and would better serve humanity, if they would focus their attention on problems such as literacy, the overabundance of violence in this society, and the lack of parental involvement in their children's lives and educations. Perhaps when they solve all those problems, they can turn a moral eye to sexual orientation, which won't need their attention any more than it does now.

Interpersonal Homophobia in the Workplace

Gay people, those thought to be gay, or people of any sexual orientation who are thought to be HIV positive or AIDS-affected are victimized in the workplace with disturbing regularity. The harassment they endure, or don't endure, runs the gamut from mental cruelty to out-and-out violence. It is not unusual for these people to receive hateful electronic mail or telephone messages. It is not unusual for gay people to read hate-filled graffiti in washrooms, or to have such messages deface their offices, cars, or other possessions. It is not unusual for gay employees to be shunned by their co-workers, or to be quietly, but continually, verbally harassed.

What is particularly disturbing about interpersonal homophobia, whether it is attributable to experiential or symbolic attitudes, is that— like most other forms of prejudice—it is continually propagated upon a minority. People are not automatically suspect, guilty, evil, sick, immoral, or inferior just because there are fewer of them . . . and people who think this way need to grow up.

Institutional Homophobia

Government, business, churches, and other institutions of society discriminate against people because of their sexual orientation in many ways. This phenomenon is known as *institutional homophobia*. Organizations and institutions set policies, allocate resources, and maintain both written and nonwritten standards for their members. In the workplace, not listing sexual orientation in a nondiscrimination policy is institutionally homophobic. Not giving equal access to benefits and resources of the organization to (same-sex) partners is too. Not using inclusive language such as *partner* or including unmarried significant others (same-sex) in invitations to corporate events is another example. Insisting that perceived cost increases, administrative complications, or outsiders are blocking the implementation of domestic partner benefits or saying that they are not needed outside of legal marriage are also all-too-frequent examples of ongoing institutional homophobia.

The bias involved in institutional homophobia is, more often than not, symbolic.

Cultural Homophobia

Heterosexism is another term for cultural homophobia, a largely unstated but prevalent belief that everyone is straight or ought to be. This standard is reinforced in almost every television show or print advertisement, where virtually every character is straight and every romantic or sexual relationship is heterosexual. This is starting to change, and there are more realistic and less stereotypical portrayals of nonheterosexuals in the media.

In the workplace, heterosexism and its symbolic bias are at the root of many of the molehills that become mountains in the minds of people who think that progressive policies toward their gay employees will be detrimental to the organization.

History proves that no system of government or commerce, from slavery in ancient Egypt to slavery in nineteenth-century North America to slavery in twentieth- and twenty-first-century developing economies, survives if it is based on the misguided belief that one group is superior to another. It cannot because people who are discriminated against are unable to give their tasks their full effort and concentration. Nor are they able to reap the full benefits of their labor. And no group of people will put up with these inabilities indefinitely, especially when it becomes clear to them that they can initiate change. For gay people, this becomes clearer every day.

Expensive and Very Bad Business

Homophobia and heterosexism in the workplace are destructive because, among other things, they cause conflict and they cost dearly. Work is a social activity as well as a serious task because it is performed by people, and people are social animals. Business relationships are the product of personal relationships, and personal relationships are the byproduct of trust and camaraderie. You do not have to like everyone you work with, but you do need to be able to get to know them well enough to know that you do not like them.

If homophobia in a workplace makes gay employees feel unable to be honest and open with co-workers about themselves or their lives, it will have a negative impact on those employees' ability to function as members of the team. They will simply not be trusted. This is what the military should be worried about in terms of "unit cohesion"—not whether someone is in mortal sexual danger from sharing a space blanket, but whether there is honesty, integrity, and respect in the ranks.

The lack of trust that results from lack of honesty and continual suppression of a person's self will affect the productivity of the work group and eventually the entire organization. Homophobia also contributes to such workplace problems as substance abuse, harassment, absenteeism, and turnover. All of these cost great sums of money.

SEXUAL ORIENTATION IN SOCIETY

In 1995, if you were to ask any human resources professional dealing with workforce diversity or employee programs what was the most difficult classification of people to include in company programs and policies, you would have been told it was the gay employee population. Call it progress or not, but it is uncertain that gay employees still hold that dubious distinction. We believe that employees wishing to organize around their religious affiliation and transgender workers are right up there, if they have not already surpassed gays in that repect.

One thing that all of these types of workplace challenges have in common is that they push the bar for what organizations are ready and able to handle within the scope of their primary mission, which is typically to make lots of money or to accomplish a specific goal. Anything that takes the eyes of the employees off that prize must be addressed.

Dealing with sexual orientation, even though it might be considered rather mainstream when compared to religion or gender identification, still is unique in terms of the elements it encompasses. First and most obviously, it encompasses the other two since a big part of conflict over sexual orientation at work is centered on religion and because transgender people are, as we said before, thrown into the mix with gays in some big vat called "sexual minorities." The term is entirely unrepresentative of what either group is dealing with, but the perception must be dealt with before we can move on to other more salient things.

In this section we examine how politics, religion, and families, as the prevailing arenas of sexual orientation in society at large, affect what happens with sexual orientation in the workplace.

Politics

The unofficial beginning of the gay civil rights movement occurred in June 1969. On the twenty-eighth day of that month, people who frequented a gay bar called the Stonewall Inn in Greenwich Village, New York, said "enough" to the harassment that they suffered on a regular basis by the city's police department. The details of the ensuing three-day riot and its short-term effects are not as important for our purposes here as are the long-term consequences of what transpired in New York City that summer.

It can be argued that a great deal of progress has been made in relation to the civil rights of gay Americans since the Stonewall riots; perhaps in no area of our lives is that more true than in civil law and politics. In a short thirty years, much has been accomplished. Not yet finished, but accomplished.

For example, in 1969, there was not a single state in which the civil rights of Americans were protected on the basis of sexual orientation. Now this is true in eleven states and over 200 cities or municipalities. In 1969, not a single jurisdiction recognized same-sex relationships for the purposes of registration for access to records or visitation rights, providing foster care to children, or being adoptive parents. Now dozens fall into one or more of these categories.

In 1969, there was no such thing as an "openly gay" politician or political appointee, and now there are members of the federal adminis- tration, members of Congress, and members of municipal government who serve and who are unabashedly gay men and women.

According to a report issued by the National Gay and Lesbian Task Force (NGLTF) at the end of 1999, within the past several years, the center of gravity has shifted from Washington, DC, to the states, and within the states, the atmosphere for antigay legislation is fading fast.[5] Opportunities exist for more and greater gains in terms of civil rights based on sexual orientation, and of course, so do opportunities for more negative rhetoric and violence against proponents for progress. This is as it ever was and how it shall ever be. Nothing worth doing is ever easy and the price of liberty is historically very high.

Highlights of the NGLTF report include the following:

- Favorable bills outnumbered unfavorable bills by 269 to 205. If one factors out bills related strictly to HIV, 214 were favorable and only 81 were unfavorable.
- More of the favorable bills progressed farther than ever before, even if they failed to win final passage.

- Among specific victories:

—Maryland's House of Delegates passed a comprehensive civil rights bill.

—South Carolina's Senate passed a hate crimes bill, as did the Texas House of Representatives.

—North Carolina and Louisiana legislative committees each passed hate crimes legislation and employment nondiscrimination measures.

—Nevada became the eleventh state with full civil rights legal protection on the basis of sexual orientation in public and private employment.

—Missouri enacted a bill adding sexual orientation and transgender people to its hate crime law.

—New Hampshire abolished its prohibition of gay adoptions, Georgia rescinded any blocking of domestic partner benefits plans being licensed in that state, and California enacted bills establishing domestic partner benefits for same-sex couples (joining Oregon and Vermont with similar provisions), banning employment and housing discrimination on the basis of orientation, and banning discrimination against gay, lesbian, bisexual, and transgender students.

Why is this happening? As stated before, because of familiarity and reason. The more we as a society engage in a serious debate and not a mudslinging exercise in futility on the subject of sexual orientation, the more progress toward inclusion can and will be made. When people come to understand sexual orientation and become acquainted with other people whose orientation differs from their own, the discrimination begins to disappear. People are reasonable for the most part; all they require is information and time to process it.

Of course, another thing driving progress in the political arena is the politicians themselves. The math is simple. If you assume that 15 percent of Americans are nonheterosexual, then you are talking about roughly 42 million Americans, probably two-thirds of whom are of voting age. That's a lot of votes, even if only 10 percent of them come out to the polls on election day.

According to the Human Rights Campaign, about 5 percent of voters identified themselves as gay when leaving the polling places in the last national elections. This is the same as the percentage of Hispanics and slightly more than Jewish voters. These numbers constitute the gay electorate as representing a significant bloc that has, for the most part, been ceded to the Democrats by the Republicans. Even that is starting to change.

The Republican rhetoric about gay Americans in the last election was nothing less than disgusting, pandering to a mean-spirited subset of our society. And it didn't get them anywhere. Although the next round of national elections is sure not to see the Republican candidates being proactive in their support of gay civil rights issues, there are a couple of cracks in the prejudicial armor that they have worn for so long.

The major Republicans won't be the ones to initiate changes in federal nondiscrimination laws, hate crimes laws, or laws concerning service in the military, but they have leaped onto the bandwagon of hiring based on merit, not on orientation. This is a major step for them; and, in fairness, more than one Republican politician, whether he or she is running for president or not, has come out in favor of the Employment Non-Discrimination Act and/or the expansion of the Hate Crimes Law (federal) to include sexual orientation. None have come out in favor of same-sex marriage or legal adoption by gay families.

The Democrats have long supported equality in civil rights on the basis of sexual orientation, stopping short of the legalization of same-sex marriage. On the Democratic side you are more likely to hear calls for expansion of existing civil rights laws, awarding domestic partner benefits for federal employees, changes in policy regarding service to one's country, and inclusion of sexual orientation in federal hate crimes and employment laws. You'll also see support for adoption rights by gay couples and for cases of second-parent adoptions in existing families. But a lot of what the Democratic candidates for major office at both the federal and state levels are calling for relative to sexual orientation was not heard from them a scant four years ago either, and so things are changing on both sides of the aisle. This again is mostly attributable to the growing visibility of, familiarity with, and awareness about sexual orientation.

It's difficult and foolhardy to pretend that what affects workplace policy relative to sexual orientation is not political and part of the broader scenario. As our public representatives debate issues such as gays in the military or same-sex marriage or ENDA, organizations of all sorts are going to have to decide where they stand on these issues because their stance will affect their ability to garner patronage and labor in exactly the same way that platforms on these issues translate into votes.

Religion

The shift from a conversation about politics to one about religion is not that far a stretch, since the word "conservative" is so closely associated these days with "religious." We have never understood this and don't understand it now. There is no hard and fast connection between a person's sexual orientation and religious fervor; nor between political inclinations and religious beliefs. It is as ridiculous to assume that all people who are Christian are also Republican as it is to assume that all gays are Democrats, and yet people seem to do so.

Religion and its place in the topic of sexual orientation in the workplace has come up previously in this book, and it will come up again when addressing specific strategies for dealing with it in conjunction with all other diversity efforts and in terms of how it is addressed responsibly in a workplace education program on sexual orientation. Here we will discuss it in terms of its general contribution to creating a less-than-inclusive workplace (*homophobic* now being understood hopefully as too simplistic a term).

Usually a religion-based argument against full inclusion in the workplace where sexual orientation is concerned will start with a very general statement such as: "The Bible says that homosexuality is wrong" (or "evil" or "a sin" or something to that effect). It is a tough place to start because what the Bible says about homosexuality is absolutely nothing, if only because the word *homosexuality* didn't exist in the centuries when the Bible was written. But if we assume, in the spirit of productive debate, that what is being referred to is a certain behavior among people, then we can reasonably answer that when it comes to interpreting Scripture, one man's prohibition is another man's license. The only thing that is clear about the Bible is that nothing in it is clear and everything in it is subject to the reader's point of view or frame of reference. Perhaps that is why so many get so much from a book written thousands of years ago by people whose life experiences have almost nothing in common with ours in the twenty-first century.

The challenge inherent in religion and sexual orientation in this society, and consequently in our workplaces, is that it is impossible to judge whose interpretation is right and what actions, if any, should be taken on the basis of that interpretation. Separation of church and state exists in the United States for a reason, which is that it is impractical to apply one sect's interpretation of morality to everybody. This is why there also exists, for the most part, separation of church and employment. When a single interpretation of morality is used to set policy for everyone in a particular place, you can bet that someone's—probably more than one someone's—rights and beliefs are going to get trampled. That is why we expound, without exception, that in the workplace, it is behavior, not beliefs, that must guide all actions.

We are not alone in thinking as we do about religion, morality, and the Bible and the interpretation of one, two, or all three of them. In Chapter 1, we referred briefly to a report called *Mixed Blessings* by Lisa Bennett, a former fellow at Harvard University's Kennedy School of Government and a writer who specializes in civil rights issues. She concludes that it only appears as if there is one religious view—a negative one—about gay and lesbian people because conservative political and religious organizations such as the Christian Coalition, the Family Research Council, and Focus on the Family have dominated the discussion in recent years. "They have done so through a combination of factors including: a significant commitment of resources; statements that, whether accurate or not, are designed to attract media attention; and a willingness to be perceived as blatantly prejudiced when it comes to lesbian and gay people."[6]

Mixed Blessings compares the position of nine major Christian denominations and four aspects of Judaism on sexual orientation and it finds little or no agreement on major points between them. And if we read the newspaper on even a casual basis these days, we see much disagreement on issues related to sexual orientation within a given denomination. In the last quarter of 1999 alone, the United Methodist Church stripped a minister of his congregation for blessing a same-sex union and, at the same time, denounced the Boy Scouts' ban on gays as discriminatory and against Methodist teaching. According to the Methodist Board of Church and Society, who asked the Boy Scouts of America to change its policy regarding gay members and scoutmasters, such a policy violates the United Methodist Book of Social Principles, which states that ". . . church members affirm the human rights and civil liberties of homosexual people."

Debate has continued literally for decades within the Methodist Church about ordination of openly gay people (they don't), or officiating at same-sex unions (some do, some don't). And the United Methodist Men group supports the Boy Scouts' policy. Which of these positions does or does not violate the United Methodist Book of Social Principles? It would clearly depend on the Methodist you were speaking to about it.

All of this constitutes an example, one of dozens we could offer, about the discrepancies within and among major religions on the topic of sexual orientation. The American Catholic Church, for example, has a much more inclusive position on sexual orientation than does the Roman Catholic Church, and Reform Jews don't see eye-to-eye on this with Conservative Jews. The point, however, is not to belabor this; the point is that there is no single point of view of "religion" as regards sexual orientation. That is what organizations must keep in mind.

Family

Two of the three most common reactions that gay people get from their families and/or friends and co-workers when they make known their nonheterosexual orientation are anger and fear. The other, just for the record, is total support.

According to sociology, anger is rooted at least in part in discomfort. Things that make us uncomfortable also have a good chance of making us angry. If there exists in a person's mind a lot of misinformation about sexual orientation—that people who are gay are sexual predators who always molest children or who engage in repulsive sexual activities, or who are by and large psychopaths damned to hell for all eternity—that person will undoubtedly feel great discomfort on the topic of sexual orientation. Then, should that person find out that his son is gay, lashing out at his own flesh and blood is not only understandable, it is downright inevitable.

But give that person information about sexual orientation that is true and dispels the myths about gays, and the discomfort will, to a great extent, go away. Yes, it is true that there will still exist a certain amount of discomfort surrounding the "sex as a verb" part of sexual orientation, but even if that level of discomfort exists, it will not be to such a degree as to make the person angry.

Fear is the other typical negative reaction to honesty about one's sexual orientation, especially from a family member or close friend. People like absolutes; they don't like ambiguity, and they fear things they don't understand. That's why honesty is the best policy when dealing with family members and the fear that might exist on both sides about that honesty.

When a person seems vehemently personally or interpersonally homophobic and he or she finds out that a well-loved family member or a well-respected friend happens to be gay, homophobia almost always disappears along with the debilitating fear of the unknown. "Individuals," someone once said, "are the enemy of stereotypes."

To our amazement and unending sorrow, there are those who have been cast out by their families due to their sexual orientation; we think this reaction is the worst manifestation of homophobia in this society. If education about sexual orientation in any workplace does nothing more than help a father not reject his gay son or help a daughter understand the compulsion felt by a mother who leaves her husband to be with her female companion, then that education has accomplished much.

Beyond the positive effects, then, that good education about sexual orientation can have on workers in the workplace, it can also, as demonstrated in the previous paragraph, improve the lives of workers outside of work and that, frankly, comes full circle to improving a worker's performance on the job.

The other consideration having to do with families that fall outside of traditional definitions, which makes organizations come face-to-face with any homophobia in their ranks, benign or otherwise, is that the family is changing legally.

The following states and districts specifically allow joint adoptions by lesbian and gay couples: Massachusetts, New Jersey, New York, Vermont, and the District of Columbia. (At this writing, California was mulling a change in status.) Two states specifically do not allow joint adoptions by lesbian and gay couples: Florida and New Hampshire. Courts in the following states have allowed joint adoptions by lesbian and gay couples (these decisions do not apply statewide): Alabama, Alaska, California, Connecticut, Illinois, Indiana, Maryland, Michigan,

Minnesota, Nevada, Oregon, Pennsylvania, Rhode Island, Texas, and Washington. In all other states, gay and lesbian couples adopt through single-parent, and then second-parent, adoptions.

In Colorado at the end of 1999, a judge in Boulder allowed two women's names on the birth certificate of their daughter. This is a decision with enormous ramifications for individuals and employers. As we'll see when we discuss domestic partner benefits and same-sex marriage in detail later in this book, homophobia at work when applied to people's families must be identified and dealt with. It is simply not a given anymore that you can have policies that don't allow for these differences in people's lives and not be called to task.

MYTHS AND FACTS

The key to disarming homophobia of any type and in any arena is to confront its myths head on. Following are some of the most common.

Myth: Being gay is a choice.

Fact: Being gay is not a choice any more than being straight is a choice. Being gay is the same as being left-handed versus right-handed or being blue-eyed versus brown-eyed. No choice is involved in any of these matters.

A person's sexual orientation is what determines to whom that person will become physically and/or emotionally attracted. The use of "and/or" is purposeful and important. What we are talking about here is not casual relationships; we are talking about extremely close relationships that manifest themselves emotionally, physically, or both. We are talking about the condition described as "falling in love." This is an experience that has emotional ramifications, physical ramifications, or both. Being in love, most people who have done it would agree, is very hard to explain, but those who have done it or are in it know it when they see it.

Gay women are attracted to women to a degree that carries the potential of falling in love with them; bisexual women are attracted to both men and women with the same potential. Gay women are not attracted to all women in a sexual or emotionally intimate way any more than straight women are attracted to all men in a sexual or emotionally intimate way.

Whether a person *behaves* in concert with his or her orientation is a completely different issue and is a decision not limited to gay people. We all decide whether to act in concert with what we know to be our own orientation, and it is the only place that choice becomes a factor in our lives as concerns our sexual orientation.

Heterosexuality is the standard for human sexual orientation and, therefore, for some people, for human sexual behavior because without a doubt, there are more heterosexual people in the world. Being the standard does not, however, make heterosexuality either morally superior or more right than other sexual orientations. It just means that the majority voted itself the standard, as majorities are wont to do.

Myth: Gays don't want to mix with other people.

Fact: Gay people are human and humans are social animals. All people, as individuals, have their own style. Some are very social and prefer to work in groups; others prefer to work alone. Whether a person is gay or straight has nothing to do with how she or he prefers to socialize.

It is obviously easier for a gay person to socialize in a safe environment than in one that is or can turn hostile. For example, imagine that every Monday morning at a given place of work there is a group that drifts over to the coffee machine to catch up with one another and discuss how they spent their weekend. Nancy is talking about her date with Bob; Bill is talking about his shopping excursion for baby furniture with his wife, Kristin; and Halette just got back from vacation with her husband, Andy.

Suzanne, a gay woman who is not open at work about her sexual orientation, is walking to the coffee machine and hears the conversation unfolding. Her company has no nondiscrimination protection on the basis of orientation, and she lives in a state and city that similarly offer no protection. She has heard her boss tell homophobic jokes and she occasionally hears others make hateful comments about "queers."

Suzanne just had a great weekend with her partner of six years, Jenny. Walking to get her coffee, she must decide whether to continue to the machine and join the conversation or make a detour and wait for everyone to disperse. Or she could go for her coffee and either pointedly not get involved in the conversation, or get involved in it but lie.

Suzanne doesn't want to lie or ignore her co-workers, so she chooses a detour. Had the environment been safe, she could have felt more comfortable approaching her co-workers and participating in the conversation to whatever level she deemed appropriate. As it is, her co-workers regard her as antisocial and not a team player. Teamwork and productivity are absolutely—and unnecessarily— negatively affected.

Whether a person wants to mix with other people is a matter of individuality and personality. Sexual orientation plays a role, usually a destructive one, in cases where gay people feel completely unsafe bringing their whole selves to work.

Myth: Nonheterosexuality is a mental illness.

Fact: Nonheterosexuality is in no way, shape, or form a mental illness. The American Psychiatric Association removed homosexuality from the *Diagnostic and Statistical Manual of Mental Disorders* close to thirty years ago. In 1999, the American Psychictric Association, American Psychological Association, and the American Psychoanalytic Association dropped any ideas or endorsement of any idea or method to try to "cure" nonheterosexuality and further dropped any restrictions on people of a nonheterosexual orientation entering their own training programs. The associations also declared in 1999 that homophobia, not homosexuality, is the real illness that people suffer from and that states should not interfere with civil marriages between gay people.

Also in 1999, a group called the Just the Facts Coalition comprising members from the American Academy of Pediatrics, the National Education Association, the American Psychological Association, and seven other groups mailed a twelve-page booklet to the heads of the 14,700 public school districts in the nation debunking the idea that homosexuality can be "cured" or that it should be cured. It also provides information that will help school administrators and educators create safe and healthy environments in which all students can achieve to the best of their ability.

Myth: All drag queens and transvestites are gay and sexual perverts.

Fact: Human sexuality characteristics pertaining to sexual orientation have nothing to do with human sexuality as it pertains to gender identification of an individual.

Transgender is often used as an umbrella term to include not only transsexuals, but intersexuals, cross-dressers, transgenderists, and others. Since transitioning transsexuals have the greatest impact on the workplace, most efforts to understand this condition in a person at work have to do with transition. But other types of transgendered people also exist in the workplace, so it is worthwhile to identify them.

Transsexuals are people whose gender identity does not match their biological sex. Male-to-female transsexuals begin life with typical male biology and identify as girls and then women. Female-to-male transsexuals start out with typical female biology and identify as boys and, later, men. Transsexuals are motivated to change their anatomy so it more closely matches their gender identity. *Transgenderists* are like transsexuals but choose not to have genital surgery. Because gender expression and sexual orientation are separate scales, transsexuals and transgenderists may be anywhere on those two continuums.

Cross-dressers are people whose gender expression is sometimes at odds with their biological sex. Most cross-dressers are males who identify primarily as men, and most are attracted to women. They dress as women on occasion and usually hope to "pass" as women on those occasions. There are also female cross-dressers who dress as men occasionally. *Transvestite* is a psychiatric term for cross-dressers, used especially for male cross-dressers who put on women's clothing for sexual excitement; most cross-dressers prefer not to be called transvestites.

Intersexuals are those whose biological sex is not typically male or female. Their gender identity, gender expression, and sexual orientation may be anywhere on those three scales.

Gay men are usually biological males who identify as men and are attracted to other biological males. Gay men who dress in women's clothing are called *drag queens*.

When we talk about transsexuals, most people think of male-to-female transsexuals, but it is important to recognize that there are also many female-to-male transsexuals. For many reasons, transsexual men do not cause as much social concern as transsexual women. It is more acceptable in our culture for women to wear men's clothing than for men to put on dresses. In fact, most male attire has been appropriated as fashionable clothing for women, including suits, tailored shirts, and ties. Some features of women's clothing, such as shoulder pads, make them look more masculine and enhance a woman's aura of authority and competence.

On the other hand, for men to wear dresses or breast padding detracts from their credibility and their status and may be considered scandalous. Most of the media attention, therefore, has been directed at transsexual women. As female-to-male transsexuals become more politically active, access medical care more frequently, and form social and political organizations, it is becoming apparent that there are roughly as many transsexual men as there are transsexual women.

In the workplace, transsexuals and transgenderists wear the same types of professional clothing that other men and women wear. Very few male cross-dressers come to work dressed as women or are interested in doing so. Their cross-dressing is something they do in the evening or on their days off or on vacation. When they are not "en femme," most cross-dressers look like ordinary men. Most intersexuals look like ordinary men and women.

Transsexuals have "normal" male or female biological sex, but their gender identity is at variance with their biological sex. Understanding what transsexual people go through is not easy for those who have never felt discomfort with their sex. For most people, gender identity has never been an issue because their sense of themselves as men or as women—their gender identity—matches their anatomy. Most people who were born female, for example, were raised as girls and were always comfortable being girls and, later, women. There may have been times when they wished they could do some of the things boys did that girls weren't allowed to, but their dissatisfaction was with the rules, not with their sex. Most people have never questioned whether their anatomical sex was right for them.

Transsexualism is a condition in which a person's sense of identity as a man or a woman does not correspond with his or her genitalia and other anatomical sexual characteristics. In other words, a person who is biologically male may feel like a woman; a person who has a female body may have a strong sense of "really" being a man.

Transsexuals are not delusional; they are aware of their actual biological sex. However, those body characteristics that signify their sex—genitalia, as well as breasts, beard, voice, etc.—feel wrong to them. It seems as though these parts don't belong and that they misrepresent who the person really is. This discomfort with their biological sex leads many transsexuals to decide to alter their bodies to make them more congruent with their inner identity.[7]

Myth: Individual civil rights applicable to the workplace are protected on the basis of gender identification.

Fact: People who do not conform to traditional gender identification modes of being enjoy even less protection than do people of a minority sexual orientation. Only one state, Minnesota, includes transgender people in its civil rights law as pertains to sexual orientation; the other ten (currently) who offer nondiscrimination protection on the basis of orientation limit it to that and do not include gender identification or nonconformity.

Four other states (Florida, New York, Oregon, and Washington) offer administrative precedent or status as a disabled person protection to persons with a gender nonconformity. And seventeen local jurisdictions offer some protection for the purposes of employment on the basis of gender nonconformity.[8]

Myth: I don't work in fashion, entertainment, or the arts, so I don't work with any gays.

Fact: In 1991, which is the last time anyone seems to have bothered to ask, *Fortune Magazine* reported that more gays work in science and engineering than in social services.[9] Forty percent more are employed in finance and insurance than in entertainment and the arts. Ten times as many work in computers as in fashion. There's no reason to think that these percentages are any different a decade later.

There are no "gay jobs." Sexual orientation has nothing to do with a person's interests, capabilities, strengths, or talents. Gay people do not choose their professions based on their sexual orientation any more than straight people do.

Myth: Gays are economically and educationally elite and therefore do not need or deserve special treatment.

Fact: Gay people are in no way economically and/or educationally elite when compared to straight people, and this argument bears an extremely uncomfortable similarity to Fascist and Nazi statements about Jews in the 1930s. That didn't come to any good at all.

Gay people are not smarter than their straight counterparts, and there isn't an institution in the country that has special acceptance rules for gays over straights. This bias about gays being intellectually superior derives from the fact that many years ago, the only way for researchers or marketers to get information from "the gay community" was to send out questionnaires to people who subscribed to magazines such as *Outlook,* or *OUT,* or *The Advocate.* The fact is that people who subscribe to magazines—any people and any magazines—are people who have the time, the money, and the intellectual interest to want to. Therefore, people who subscribe to magazines, everything from *Newsweek* to *Fishermen's Weekly,* are typically in a higher income bracket and have completed more years of formal education than the average. Whether this makes them either economically or intellectually elite is seriously questionable.

As for gays wanting "special rights," implying a desire for rights over and above what other people enjoy, there is no truth to that at all. The rights that are being lobbied for are in the spirit of equal rights with heterosexuals in all matters pertaining to our societal responsibilities and privileges, our families, and our employment. We are even willing to pay the "marriage tax" if only the rest of society would let us.

Myth: Gays should not work with children under any circumstances.

Fact: There is absolutely no evidence to suggest that gay people should not work with, advise, counsel, or parent children. All evidence is to the contrary. Gays do not "recruit" and they do not have a secret, pervasive desire to molest children. The first concept is nothing short of silly since you cannot recruit into a sexual orientation; and the second is so obnoxious and disgusting that it warrants no further comment except this one: More than 90 percent of sexual abuse and child molestation is perpetrated against children (typically girls) by heterosexual adult males who are usually members of their own families or who are known to them. Pedophilia is a psychosis, and pedophiles need serious help; neither they, nor the condition, nor the victims benefit from use as a self-serving instrument of hate.

Women, especially gay women, almost never sexually molest children, and data also suggest that many men who victimize young boys do not self-identify as gay. In fact, many male abusers of boys are married, with long heterosexual histories.[10] People's fear of gays working with children is the result of tabloid sensationalism spewed by those with the nerve to stand on pulpits of morality. They ought to be ashamed of themselves.

Myth: I can always tell if a person is gay.

Fact: There are no distinguishing characteristics of gay people that set them apart physically, emotionally, intellectually, or spiritually from straight people. No skin color, no hairstyle, no eye color, no fashion, no mannerism, or anything else identifies a person as gay or straight. You cannot tell whether a person is gay just by looking at her or him. The only way to know for sure is to ask.

Similarly, you cannot accurately judge a person's potential behavior or abilities by his or her sexual orientation once known. Sexual orientation has nothing at all to do with a person's ability to teach, to police, to soldier, to construct, to mop up, to play football, to dance, to write, or to do anything else.

Myth: If a gay person comes out to me and I don't approve, I have to pretend that I do.

Fact: If a person tells you that he or she is gay, you should respond honestly. If that means you don't approve, then you should feel free to say so. If you are able to be supportive of his or her efforts at work or otherwise even though you don't approve, you should feel free to say that. If it is *homosexual sexual behavior* that is problematic for you, you should have no qualms about expressing that opinion in an appropriate way. A great deal of progress can be made if people pay more attention to the fact that although they may have a problem with sex as a verb (regardless of who's doing it) in much the same way that they have a problem with violent behavior, it is the behavior they object to, not the person.

If you wish to express your disapproval of certain behaviors, it is well within your rights to do so. But you should endeavor to remember that this opinion does not mitigate in the least your responsibility to allow others to be who they are, free from discrimination and irrational hatred.

Chapter 4

Specific Strategies
for Inclusion of Sexual Orientation
in the Workplace

People do not work at their best if they work in fear. But prevalent homophobia and heterosexism in the workplace make it true that, as of this writing, many gay people hide their sexual orientation and stay in the closet. There is not a GLBTS (gay, lesbian, bisexual, transgender, straight) employee group that we've worked with anywhere in the United States in the last five years that doesn't maintain two membership list—one for those who are openly involved, attend meetings and symposiums and take on action items, and one for those who want to remain informed and who get involved on a very carefully chosen case-by-case basis. *All* of the closeted employees we have interacted with admitted worrying daily about being found out, to the extent that it affects their performance every day. This is not good for the individual or for the organization. Hiding takes energy and time—energy and time that should be spent on the task at hand.

A principal goal of any organization should be to create a culture in which each employee has the opportunity to make a full contribution and to advance on the basis of performance. Hiding forces gay employees to lead a double life, to pretend that the things that motivate them to succeed on the job—their partners, their families, their homes, their interests—don't exist. Organizations that continue to exclude segments of their workforce risk sending the message that some people are less valued, less important, and less welcome.

HIDING IN PLAIN SIGHT

Consider this for a moment. What would everyone do if gays couldn't hide? Women and racial minorities, who are also historically victims of workplace discrimination, do not have the luxury of hiding even if they wanted to. If gays couldn't hide, just as people of color and women cannot hide, then all the questions surrounding them would come to a head that much faster.

It is the sheer ability of gay people to hide, to blend in, that makes some people believe that we choose to be as we are (because we can hide it practically on demand), and makes others believe that our arguments for equal rights are not as valid as those coming from people whose circumstances make it impossible to hide, as if logically it mattered. It has really become a "damned if you do, damned if you don't" Catch-22 situation. And it has become untenable for most gay people to continue playing the game. There are two reasons. One, it is a losing game for the participant no matter what; it is unhealthy, unsafe, and a waste of time and energy. Two, as more people come out, especially in the workplace, and gain victories in equal employment provisions among other things, it encourages more people to come out. The people who led the way at Stonewall were undoubtedly courageous trendsetters. But thirty-odd years later, millions have walked in those shoes and have mostly lived to tell about it with optimism.

Being in the closet means censoring thoughts, words, and actions relative to one's sexual orientation for different audiences. A gay man may be in the closet to his family, but not to his co-workers—or only to some of them. Perhaps a gay woman's brother knows the truth of her sexual orientation, but another brother, two sisters, her parents, and all the aunts, uncles, and cousins—save one who lives in Alaska—don't know. It can all be quite a handful to manage, and it quickly becomes unmanageable, which is a large part of the reason that, in short order, many gay people stop trying.

Don't believe us? Try it yourself. See if you can go through a whole day without doing, saying, demonstrating, wearing, displaying, or commenting upon anything that would send a signal about your sexual orientation to any other person that you come into contact with. Most straight people can't go twenty minutes until their first slip. Give it a sincere try.

Most straight people don't understand the closet because they've never been in it. Because heterosexuality is the order of things, they say that gays who come out go too far, making an issue of their sexuality. And because straights have never experienced the closet, they think that coming out is the hardest thing. What they don't realize is that *the real pain is in being in the closet, not coming out of it.*[1]

As Jonathan Rauch wrote once in *The Wall Street Journal,* "any [workplace or governmental] policy insisting that gays lead secret lives is futile, inhumane, and unrealistic. Because fewer gays are willing to hide, the old deal—gays pretending to be straight and straights pretending to believe them—is off."[2]

As the twenty-first century begins, it is undeniably easier to be out of the closet in many parts of the United States and Canada than it was at the beginning of our lives. And the necessity of being out and being accepting for both individuals and organizations is tantamount to absolute. When looking for a job, more young people are asking themselves, "Will the new work environment be supportive of me as a member of an orientation or gender identification minority?" Most universities have nondiscrimination policies that are fully inclusive and most of the top business schools in the United States, including many state systems, have domestic partner benefits. Today, more graduating students are out of the closet than ever before and they won't be going back in. If they feel that a certain employer will force them back into the closet through subtle but exclusionary practices, they will go somewhere else to work. The competition for labor is much too intense for an organization to think it can make employees continue to play this game of hide-and-seek.

WHAT CAN ORGANIZATIONS DO?

An organization cannot and should not mandate that gay employees come out; that is a very personal decision for each individual who has cause to confront it. Rather, the organization can take time to understand: (1) what it means for a person to come out, and (2) the process by which the organization itself comes out.

Several models dealing with individual coming out have been developed primarily by psychologists and sociologists, and some do a good job of providing a general framework for what is always, again, a very personal process and set of circumstances. No one way of coming out is right or more right than any other way.

What these models are good for is giving language to the process so that people can manipulate the models as they see fit. For instance, gay people who are considering coming out can realize that what they are feeling is not unique to them, which can help them overcome terrifying feelings of isolation. Many have gone before; many will come out after. And perhaps straight people can use the information to better understand how a gay colleague or family member is feeling and why.

Of the models we have studied, we identify most with Vivienne Cass's "Homosexuality Identity Formation: A Theoretical Model" originally published in 1979.[3] Although its name could stand to be updated, the model itself has held up well over the decades. Where we part company with her is in the matter of scope. She limits the discussion to the process that the individual goes through; we believe there is also a process of organizational coming out that is at least as important, if not more important, to consider when dealing with sexual orientation in the workplace. Yes, individuals are the enemies of stereotype, and individuals drive change, and individuals must have a sense of self before they will be able to drive change, but if they don't also know where the organization is relative to its own "coming out" about sexual orientation, then their efforts will be fraught with failure.

The organization comes to accept that its gay employees who are able to be open enhance the productivity and profitability of the organization. And because the organization is nothing more than a collection of individuals, the process of the organization catching on to this concept is really no more than each individual accepting it and passing it along, sort of a human domino effect. When the organization comes out, becomes fully incorporated as we will explain in a moment, it becomes a more fulfilling environment for all concerned.

Coming Out for the Individual

An individual who decides to come out may go through a series of phases, as follows. Again, keep in mind that this is a generalization of a very individualistic process.

Phase 1: Comparison

In the comparison phase, people compare things they see, hear, feel, and know about themselves with input concerning nonheterosexual sexual orientation and begin to make connections. The more this personalization happens, the more likely they are to begin to reassess their own sexuality. This period of reassessment is necessary because most people make the mistake early in their lives of believing that everyone is just like everyone else—which is, of course, nonsense. This nonsense becomes dangerous when some begin to believe that certain people are better than others.

The comparison phase is a deeply introspective part of a person's life. During it, self-alienation can quickly become social alienation as people first struggle to come to grips with what they are feeling and learning about themselves and then try to decide how they are going to deal with it in relation to everyone else in their lives.

Some people never make it through either the self-alienation or the social alienation. It is not unusual for gays to try to devalue the truth about themselves and bury it in an attempt to be "normal," to live up to their family's expectations, to keep in line with their religious convictions, or for any number of self-deprecating reasons. Many gays get married and have children as a way to prove that they are "normal." They can live their whole lives in this fashion but will always know that there is a part of themselves they are not acknowledging.

At work, people stuck in the comparison phase who are trying to put it aside may be very resentful of those gay people who don't hide who they are, and they may be among the most vocal in their opposition to anything that tries to value gay relationships at the same level as straight relationships. These people are undoubtedly under a lot of stress and can be among the most disruptive of employees.

Employers are well advised to understand that homophobia can come from gay and bisexual people as much as it can come from straight, "conservative" people. Fostering an environment that encourages duplicity and secrecy is expensive. Hiding mechanisms that employees use include substance and alcohol abuse, absenteeism, tardiness, conflicts with others, and turnover. These things do nothing to enhance the bottom line.

Phase 2: Support

A successful transition out of Phase 1 leads to a phase of support, resulting from the change from tolerance to acceptance to support. Tolerance and acceptance, as stated before, are not automatically good;

tolerance or acceptance of something is just putting up with it. By implication, when you tolerate something you would rather not have to deal with it. Worse, people do not make any effort to understand the things they tolerate and they often accept things just because they are told to.

But it is important for a gay person coming out to first be able to tolerate and then accept the fact that she or he is gay. Coming out is a process, and a refusal to at least tolerate a situation signals a refusal to enter into the process of resolving it one way or the other.

The point of the support phase is to move beyond tolerance and mere acceptance and to ultimately become wholly supportive of one's sexuality . . . or someone else's. We say this because there is a potential for a lot of anger directed toward "the straight world" by gay people moving through Phase 2 of coming out. Part of successfully completing this phase is to stop seeing straight people and everything they do and represent as the enemy.

Once people are able to deal with sexual orientation as it really is, to go beyond the irrational fears and unsubstantiated myths (about people of any orientation), they can support whatever their own or someone else's happens to be. This is a crucial step in maintaining mental health and self-esteem. From here, people decide how they are going to make their place in the world.

Phase 3: Incorporation

In the last phase of individual coming out, mere support gives way to pride and full-blown sense of incorporation in terms of understanding the ramifications of human sexuality and being able to make connections with the rest of the world because of it.

We use the word *incorporation* deliberately to describe the process of bringing one set of characteristics in line with another. Many prefer the word *integrate,* meaning "to make into a whole by joining with something else."

Our difficulty with *integration* when applied to sexual orientation is the implication that people of other than heterosexual orientation must be in some way joined or related to heterosexuals in order to be whole. This is not the case at all. Both gays and straights are already whole and don't require integration of another set of characteristics to make them so.

We believe that incorporation is a goal of coming out when it is defined as "the ability, fostered by understanding, to unite different characteristics." People who are united within themselves are better able to function in the workplace or any place. By coming out, gay people allow straight people to see, experience, and appreciate more of the characteristics they have in common and less of what differentiates them, which, in truth, is not much at all.

People with a strong and positive sense of self are valuable employees. They are productive, forthright, clear-minded, and outspoken independent thinkers. They are also at the point where others may accuse them of "flaunting their sexuality," and conflicts may begin in earnest. The employer must appreciate the journey that these people have made to get to the self-affirming place where they are. Such understanding will allow the enterprise to harness the individual's positive energy appropriately. Such understanding is the result of the organization coming out too.

Organizational Coming Out

It is our opinion that most leaders of most organizations disapprove of discrimination against their gay employees. We also believe that most professionals in the area of human resources/training and development do not support discrimination against their gay co-workers but that many are hesitant to take a leadership position in proactively ensuring that such discrimination does not occur. But frankly, and usually to our dismay, we have also met HR/diversity and training personnel who don't understand a need to include sexual orientation in their initiatives and worse, who don't think it should be included.

It is the role of an HR/diversity or organization development professional to be able to represent the requirements of all co-workers, and to do so proactively before trouble occurs. If professionals do not see the need to include sexual orientation in these efforts, then they have an obligation to learn more about the subject to be able to do their jobs. If they feel that their personal value or belief systems preclude them from being able to find ways to balance their beliefs with their professional responsibilities regardless of how much information they are given, and if they are unable to live up to all facets of the organization's nondiscrimination policies, then they need to find another line of work.

For those who do see the logic in full inclusion and who are able to balance their personal and professional responsibilities, there are phases to go through too.

Phase 1: Acknowledgment

Gay people exist in every workplace. There are gay doctors, gay pilots, gay stockbrokers, gay lawyers, gay teachers, gay athletes, gay everybodies. In the acknowledgment phase, the organization states both verbally and in writing that it knows there are gay people in the world. In other words, it stops saying, "We don't have any issues of sexual orientation to deal with because no gays are working here."

Organizational acknowledgment carries with it the same positive force as an individual's acknowledgment of his or her own orientation or of someone else's. It says, "I acknowledge your existence, and although I might not always agree with you or even like you, I will not pretend that you are not here."

Phase 2: Accommodation

In the accommodation phase, the organization as a unit and all its individual cogs agree that specific provisions must be made to support their acknowledgment. So they begin to do things such as offer partner benefits to same-sex (and possibly to unmarried opposite-sex) couples. They use inclusive language in their communications, substituting the word *partner* for *spouse*. They reprimand (and mean it) those who discriminate against or harass their fellow co-workers; they put gay members on appropriate task forces; and they recognize gay employee groups (if other employee groups are similarly recognized). In short, they back up their acknowledgment with concrete action whenever possible.

In this phase, the employer may have to be lobbied to be inclusive, but once asked (or thrice asked), the employer will.

Phase 3: Incorporation

In the final phase of organizational coming out, the employer does not need to be asked anymore, and no individual working there has to wonder at all what is expected regarding his or her behavior toward gay co-workers.

Incorporation in an organization is just like incorporation in an individual. Sexual orientation is a fact of life. It just is. It is the result of a completely internalized understanding of the fact that people are people with lots of differing characteristics, of which sexual orientation is just one. An incorporated organization, again, like an individual, is one that keeps its value judgments to an absolute minimum and strives to build in proactive correction systems for those times when negative judgments are made despite the best efforts to avoid them.

Such organizations are marked by their progressive, proactive stances as reflected in everything they do. These organizations, as Shell Oil makes clear in its diversity documents, fully understand that an entity is only as healthy as each of its parts, and they will do everything they can to promote the well-being of every individual they take under their wing as employee or as customer.

Coming Out Is a Process

Coming out is a process for both individuals and organizations, just as education is a process. A person's ability to come out is in direct correlation to his or her perception of level of competence and his or her perceived level of value and worth in the marketplace . . . and self-esteem. The same is true of an organization.

As we have said before, the decision to come out or not is intensely personal. It cannot be mandated; it can hardly be suggested. However, homophobia in all its manifestations would be greatly reduced if more people only knew how many of their friends, acquaintances, co-workers, and family members are not heterosexual. To the extent that every person—and organization—in the world will be able to go through the entire process described here, there will be (1) no more closeted gay people, (2) no more discriminatory workplaces, and (3) no more homophobia.

These are lofty goals, to be sure, and difficult. But they are attainable. We are not naive, but if people did not believe in the indefatigable capacity for things to improve, for understanding to become more widespread, for positive change to occur eventually, and for people to be better tomorrow than they are today, no one would get up in the morning.

SPECIFIC STRATEGIES FOR FULL INCLUSION

The organization can do many things, big and small, cheap or expensive, to secure and maintain the best effort of its employees. In return for these gestures, programs, and policies, the employer has the right to expect dedication, loyalty, self-motivation, and cooperation from all employees at all times. From a gay employee's perspective, the trade is a simple one. Gays want the same as is expected by and granted to heterosexual employees without question or comment: a safe working environment, equitable benefits, and appropriate public support.

What follows are specific strategies that can ensure that this bargain between employees and employers is well kept:

• Nondiscrimination policies
• Education programs
• Domestic partner benefits
• Employee/management alliances
• Brown bag meetings
• Utilizing change agent methodologies
• Dealing with spirituality/religion
• Mentoring and coming-out coaches
• Internal and external community outreach initiatives
• Developing and maintaining internal informational resources

Nondiscrimination Policies

An inclusive nondiscrimination policy is the most important thing the organization must have. A policy that stipulates without ambiguity that in all facets of employment, people will be treated no differently—no better and no worse—than their co-workers on the basis of their sexual orientation or gender identification is an absolute necessity.

As described in some detail in Chapter 2, the overwhelming majority of North Americans favor fully inclusive nondiscrimination workplace policies and the same majority doesn't know that such protection is not "automatic." According to the HRC, only 14 percent of people realize that it is still completely legal in forty states to fire people based on their real or perceived sexual orientation, so what people believe is fair and in force in fact is not. Every organization on this continent could contribute to rectifying this misunderstanding with little or no effort, money, or downside by simply adding the appropriate language to their nondiscrimination policies and explaining why to their own employees.

Even the federal government of the United States (Canada having progressed a bit farther at this writing) has adopted these standards of protection for federal workers in the form of a report from the Office of Personnel Management called "Addressing Sexual Orientation Discrimination in Federal Civilian Employment."[4]

This guide, issued in response to President Clinton's historic executive order prohibiting discrimination based on sexual orientation in the federal civilian workplace, offers specific avenues for federal employees to address discrimination, including referring matters to the Merit Systems Protection Board or the Office of Special Counsel, and using the negotiated grievance procedure, and the agency grievance procedure.

What's missing from Clinton's order, and from the law of the land in the United States, is inclusion of sexual orientation in EEO mandates that would lend it quite a bit more weight in terms of both adherence and the effectiveness of grievance procedures. Absent this status, the executive order's protection is very iffy indeed and, for that reason, there is continued lobbying for the Employment Non-Discrimination Act, which would provide federal job protection (with weight of law) to all people in the United States regardless of sexual orientation, real or perceived.

As a strategy to signal commitment to full inclusion, all organizations can sign a statement endorsing ENDA, and can also consider endorsing federal hate crimes legislation.[5]

Even if companies such as ExxonMobil think it is sufficient not to include sexual orientation in their nondiscrimination policies and say that it's included anyway, the truth is, it's not. If a policy doesn't include those exact words, then it's not in there. And the words must be *sexual orientation,* not *lifestyle* and not *preference.* Neither lifestyles nor preferences have anything whatsoever to do with sexual orientation and little to do with work in general.

If your organization does not currently include the words *sexual orientation* in its nondiscrimination policy, there are steps you can take to persuade it otherwise. (*Note:* If the words in the policy are *preference* and/or *lifestyle* instead of *orientation,* the same strategies of complete understanding and enlisting support on a peer level are still necessary.)

- Get a copy of the existing policy, review it with members of a gay/straight employee group, and make sure that it is completely understood. If no such group exists, review it with like-minded individual employees.
- If other employee groups are sanctioned by the company, go to their meetings and try to enlist their support for the language change.
- Try to identify a "champion" in senior management at the company who is willing to listen to and then represent your concerns to the person who can change the policy. Be prepared to have several discussion with this person so that she or he is fully armed with the facts needed to solicit the change.
- Focus on the business case; if it were just a matter of right versus wrong, it would have happened already.

Education Programs

There is absolutely no doubt in our minds that the single best thing an organization can do to accommodate sexual orientation in the workplace, once it's been acknowledged by way of the nondiscrimination policy, is to design, develop, and deliver to *everyone* in the organization *no matter how long it takes* a program of education focused on sexual orientation in the workplace.

This topic is worthy of, and gets, its own chapter. Please refer to Chapter 5 for more about this extremely important strategic element of inclusion.

Domestic Partner Benefits

For a number of reasons, the implementation of DPBs has taken on a life of its own both in terms of symbolic importance of full inclusion and in terms of the amount of information necessary—and available—to implement them. Therefore, this topic is also worthy of, and gets, its own chapter. Please refer to Chapter 6 for everything you want and need to know about DPBs.

Employee/Management Alliances

Employee groups of any kind allow people with similar interests or characteristics to interact with others who are like them. In the case of a group formed around sexual orientation, the existence of such a group may serve to help individuals know that they are not alone. Feeling like "the only one" is a depressing condition common to many gay workers.

For any of these strategies we're outlining to actually occur, of course, there must be the buy-in and support of management. And we've found that the best way to engender both is to form what were typically called employee groups, employee networks, or employee alliances as a "gay/straight/trans/bi employee-management alliance" (GSTBEM alliance). We think a lot of people forget that management are employees too, with as much an equal stake in what transpires as anyone else at the company. And, truth be told, some managers are not heterosexual either. The best way, therefore, for these people to be involved in what's going on is to be actually involved in what's going on.

A prevalent fear about employee groups of any kind has, for the longest time, been that they would begin to constitute a lobby or a union for their specific demands and that they would prove more divisive to and engender more conflict in a given workplace. So it's better to start off such an effort with a spirit of cooperation, and that means inviting management to cooperate.

Organizations as diverse as Shell, AT&T, Ford Motor Company, Motorola, and literally hundreds if not thousands of others have chosen a model whereby a member of management, typically senior management, assumes the role (almost always voluntarily) as the principal liaison between the group and the company. This strategy has a lot going for it, not the least of which is that if most people in an organization see a member of senior management behaving in a particular way, they will be encouraged to act that way too.

There are other reasons to champion a GSTBEM alliance. One is that formation of such a group gives an effective and responsible voice to the concerns of the entire employee population, since all orientations and identifications should be represented. If HR staff members, for example, don't know what to do to help their gay employees feel safer and able to be more productive, maybe it's because no gay person knows how to reach out and tell them and they don't know how to ask. Such a group is an incredible two-way communications vehicle.

A second benefit of these groups reaches way beyond just the gay or transgender workers. Such groups can lead to more productive dialogues about this issue and can help create a sense of community for potentially alienated workers. This strategy does not apply only to gays in the workplace; many people have gay friends and family members they feel protective of or in conflict about. Their feelings can just as easily negatively impact their job performance.

Third, such groups always have constituted a tremendous resource to help the organization understand what potential exists for their products and/or services to the "gay market." Certainly one of the most positive aspects of awareness and openness about orientation from a strictly dollars-and-cents standpoint, as we've discussed, is that a whole untapped market is ready, willing, and able to patronize organizations willing to meet them halfway. Telling the organization where this halfway point is and how the organization can get there is a powerful strength of an employee/management alliance.

Setting an Alliance Up

In terms of setting up employee/management alliances in general, the organization should consider the following:[6]

1. What is the business case?
2. Is there a clear mission statement and set of objectives?
3. Can organizational facilities be used?

4. Are there guidelines for the group to operate within that are consistent with the mission of the organization as a whole?
5. Will funding be provided or will the groups be self-funded?

In terms of starting a GSTBEM alliance in particular, here are some steps to consider:[7]

1. Know what the organization will and will not allow. By all means, research the organization's position on sexual orientation in particular and on employee groups in general. Your proposal for a group should be fully in line with those guidelines.
2. Expand outreach about the group's formation and/or existence using every method available to you from word of mouth to electronic communications to listings in the local papers. Consider using an anonymous e-mail drop, a P.O. box, or an answering machine for RSVPs for as long as such precautions are felt necessary. No one need be a poster child for sexual orientation in a given workplace.
3. Be sure to respect your members' differing levels of comfort with having their orientation or gender identification known. Efforts to make everyone feel as safe as possible in coming out are paramount to the mission of the group (typically), but this comes to all in their own time and must be accommodated. People who are willing to work only behind the scenes for a while are still willing to work.
4. Network and ally yourself with other similar alliances in your vicinity and especially with the other alliances at your organization. Many goals of alliances are alike and will be gained faster if you work together and not linearly.
5. Frame all your discussions in terms of total quality management, maximum productivity, enhancing profitability, respect for individuals, best effort, and the like. In other words, focus always on the business case. It's the only case that matters to business.

Brown Bag Meetings

In addition to formal education programs on sexual orientation in the workplace that are part of a full-blown diversity education curriculum (see Chapter 5), the organization can, and many do, offer less formal "brown bag" meetings or presentations about orientation and human health issues at work.

In general, we all know, of course, that the first rule of a successful meeting is to make sure that food will be served. Brown bag meetings are, typically, lunchtime or extended lunchtime meetings, and there is nothing wrong with doing a program on sexual orientation in this way. But note the following:

- It should be more of a presentation than a workshop, although not very formal.
- It must have the same level of structure and preparation as a formal presentation even if it doesn't look or feel like one. It is a horrific mistake to put such a meeting in the hands of an unskilled or unprepared facilitator. Because of the sense of casualness about brown bags, people actually feel more free to act out and try to disrupt them (if that is their focus); or to simply interrupt and try to get a debate or even just a discussion going.
- You must ensure that the goals and objectives for the meeting are as clear as they are in a workshop and they must be laid out from the start. And, as with a workshop, there must be a set beginning and ending time. We recommend that people not be allowed to come and go freely, but to expect to stay for the whole event so that nothing is heard out of context.
- At least one member of senior management should be present. The event must be sanctioned and officially supported as much as a full-scale education program is perceived to be by most employees. This is sometimes difficult for people who are somewhat closeted to accept, but it's a very important first step in creating an environment that supports open dialogue which will lead, hopefully, eventually to an environment that feels safe to everyone all the time.
- Some workshop-type exercises can be used at these less structured events; it's also a great opportunity to get a willing member of the employee alliance to talk about what it's like to be who she or he is at that place. This is very effective, but again, should be done in a structured context with a skilled facilitator ready to assist that person.

Change Agent Strategies

There is a philosophy within the discipline of diversity that is called "being a change agent." Change agent strategies are said to be either proactive or reactive, and when applied to sexual orientation, they include the following.

Proactive

1. Educate yourself about sexual orientation in order to formulate, and where necessary express, a position that balances one's own opinion with the change agent behavior encouraged by the organization.
2. Try to avoid heterosexist assumptions; that is, don't assume that everyone you work with or come into contact with is heterosexual.
3. Share anything you've learned about human sexuality and homophobia that might encourage others to adopt productive behaviors.
4. Use inclusive language (e.g., "partner" instead of "husband" or "wife") whenever possible in all communications.
5. Encourage gay co-workers to be part of the social groups you form at work, including bringing their partners to functions when appropriate.
6. Take time to understand the local laws and ordinances that relate to sexual orientation—especially your organization's nondiscrimination policies. If you have questions about these policies, ask.
7. If you have questions about orientation, use organizational resources or resources in your town or city to get answers. Only with information can people make informed decisions.
8. Display items in your workspace such as books, magnets, or posters that demonstrate your awareness of inclusiveness.

Reactive

1. If someone asks you a question or confronts you with an opinion about sexual orientation in the workplace that you feel unprepared for, feel free to say that you don't know how to

respond, but that you will get back to them. Then reach out to the organizational resources available to you so that you can respond in a meaningful and helpful way that both parties will feel good about.

2. Refuse to laugh at antigay "humor."
3. Cite company policy about nondiscrimination, or simply walk away from a group that is indulging in verbal discrimination. If you feel comfortable doing so, personalize the issue by saying, "I know gay people and what you just did/said offends me."
4. Encourage other people to read books or attend education sessions on orientation in order to hear other points of view if they seem particularly troubled by the issue.

Any and all of these can be utilized by individuals and groups who are working to create a more inclusive workplace.

Dealing with Spirituality/Religion

According to a cover story in *BusinessWeek*, a spiritual revival of sorts is sweeping across America, and more than being about "religion" in the sense of "God," it's about faith in oneself, about meditation, and about using spirituality in a career.[8] As detailed in Bennett's report that we alluded to earlier, effective public relations efforts might force us to conclude that a single, fundamentalist and deeply conservative school of thought is driving the conversation about religious convictions insofar as sexual orientation is concerned, but that appears not to be the case. Religion at work is more accurately described as "spirituality at work," and it is not only about exclusion or conflict at all.

Organizations should not fear this renewed sense of faith or spirituality in their workplaces any more than they should fear new awareness or visibility of sexual orientation. Harnessing the power that drives both are potential sources of strength, productivity, and profitability for the organization if it doesn't allow zealots to dominate.

What's happening relative to spirituality at work may be no more than a reflection of broader trends, according to the article in *Business-Week;* we agree and present it as something to consider as useful in terms of sexual orientation in the workplace. Statistics indicate that people are working the equivalent of one month more each year than they did ten years ago and therefore the workplace is becoming the social gathering spot that the temple or the church or the local tavern used to be. The office is where more people eat, exercise, meet possible partners, and drop their kids and even their laundry.[9] And the greater diversity of the workplace population also means better exposure to different ways of being spiritual, thus providing people with very interesting things to share.

At the same time, what organizations are doing to appeal to potential labor and patronage on the basis of orientation or any other diversity factor also applies to being the kind of employer or provider that upholds and respects personal values. This doesn't mean throwing all the corporate resources only at the feet of the mean-spirited, self-serving, or exclusionary elements that hide behind a curtain of "religion" or "morality" or "family values." It means offering people at work a real sense of meaning and fulfillment about what they do because that's what people are saying that they want from work. Money is just not enough.

Last, organizations that are working hard to see to this need in their workers are benefiting from evidence which proves that such things not only soothe workers' psyches but also deliver improved productivity. This is not just a fad.[10]

It's not hard to see what these two efforts or alliance groups might have in common: a desire to get more out of the working experience, a desire to be able to be true to themselves and their ideals, and the desire to be able to openly discuss matters of import that concern them without fear of retribution.

Instead of fearing what might happen should such alliances as a GSTB and a spirituality group form, perhaps efforts should be made to ensure that both simply live up to the alliance requirements as outlined above, that both are fully inclusive of all opinions within the range of their charter, and that both are ready, willing, and able to engage in meaningful dialogue about their issues of mutual concern to the betterment of the organization and all who work there.

Mentoring and Coming-Out Coaches

Over the last decade, mentoring has established itself as an effective and respected mechanism to leverage the strengths of individuals in the workplace. The concept of mentoring is simple. A person who is already established, usually in a high management position, takes a specific individual (perhaps more than one) under her or his wing and personally monitors and contributes to that individual's advancement. When applied to diversity, however, mentoring takes on additional meaning.

Instead of one-to-one mentoring, we advocate that organizations explore a system of corporate mentoring in which team-to-team replaces one-to-one guidance. The idea behind corporate mentoring is that it brings qualified individuals, regardless of race, gender, orientation, or what have you into the executive level by extending the concept to whole groups instead of just to individuals. This is a merit system rather than a predictive one.

In a predictive mentoring system (one-to-one), certain assumptions are made about the person's ability. In corporate mentoring, there are no subjective predictions; there is only performance. And the responsibility for bringing people along is not left to one person with one set of standards or viewpoints, but rather is shared by a team of managers bringing to the table diverse standards and viewpoints.

Insofar as sexual orientation is concerned, in our approach it is much easier to have a gay presence as a mentor or as a protégé, even if one or both are closeted. We sincerely hope that an organization will have a gay manager qualified to be a mentor, because his or her presence both in the process and on the management team certainly sends the correct message that people are judged by their work and not by their orientation. But if no such person is visible at your organization, then consider alternatives such as looking outside your organization for a qualified civic leader, consultant, or professor to participate (and hopefully help encourage someone to step up to the plate from the home team).

We advocate a similar strategy for sending the right message in your ranks, which we call "coming-out coaches." Although this term may be new to some, the concept has been around in an underground fashion for many years.

Coming-out coaches are people who have themselves come out at the office, worked through whatever difficulties that engendered, and now feel comfortable enough and ready to help others who are struggling with the same decisions. These people are not advocates of coming out in terms of trying to talk people into it, nor are they qualified psychological counselors. They are just regular employees who lend support simply by their willingness to attest to the fact that "I did it and you can do it, too."

Human resources managers can help promote such an informal network of coaches in their own workplaces, and help it to grow by making it available to neighboring enterprises. And of course, the employee alliance is the number one source for providing people willing to serve in this role for others. Both mentoring and coming-out coach strategies are hugely cooperative efforts between the alliance and the organization.

Community Outreach Initiatives

Community outreach, used internally, means things such as ensuring that all communication uses inclusive language and that all people, regardless of background, are made to feel welcome. It means supporting the constructive efforts of a sanctioned group by making sure they have the same access to budget and technology as do other employee networks. In too many organizations with whom we've worked, the women's coalition, to use a broad example, is a national effort, while the gay/straight alliances operate regionally. The message being sent here is clear to those involved, and it speaks of a basic hypocrisy of policy that eats away at the ability to make progress. If all your employee alliances are regional, fine; but if they are all national except one or two, then that is not fine.

Internal Outreach

Internal outreach also means doing everything possible to encourage participation by all types of people in the organization and going out of the way, perhaps far out of the way, to provide a safe environment where closeted gay people can come out or participate at any level they deem safe. Again, we've worked with too many organizations in which nonheterosexuals at the headquarters facilities or in urban centers feel affirmed, valued, and able to be out while their co-workers at more distant facilities literally work and live in fear for their lives.

External Outreach

Externally, community outreach means getting involved in the communities in which you operate. It means supporting local organizations such as PFLAG[11] or endorsing ENDA to Congress. Allow your employees to participate in community speaking programs and/or to work in support of meals-on-wheels programs or the fight against breast and ovarian cancer. Put more than your money out there; give people the opportunity to represent you in these causes in their community. The PR you'll get from this will be well worth the negligible expense.

Developing and Maintaining Internal Informational Resources

Finally, make sure there is a resource room or kiosk or person who is up to speed on the situation relative to sexual orientation in every single facility that you maintain. People on all sides of the question need to have a place to go to get information instead of letting their concerns fester and eat away at their confidence and ability to perform their jobs.

Such a room or referral service should be set up so that either can be accessed anonymously if an individual desires, although hopefully soon such anonymity won't be considered necessary. Such resources may be limited to existing employee assistance programs (EAPs) or could also include listings of literature available on the subject at hand, statistical information about sexual orientation, and names and phone numbers of organizations of all kinds—from clergy to political to family-focused or legal—that offer support or information mechanisms.

The organization can also use a consultant. Consultants can provide a single information source, or can refer employees to groups, counselors, schools, and other organizations that have expertise in the employee's area of concern.

Supplementary Programs

Additional strategies that the organization may want to consider spearheading include the following:

- A hot line to report all forms of harassment and discrimination including, but not necessarily limited to, sexual orientation
- A system of accountability for a nonhostile work environment by division, work group, business unit, geography, or other criteria
- Expansion of existing reward/award programs to include recognition of superior efforts to engender a safer, better working environment for all—perhaps with an emphasis on sexual orientation
- Encouragement for gay employees to bring their partners to appropriate enterprisewide events, or to display (again, appropriately as others do) items from their personal lives

While the organization and individuals therein work through these processes of coming out and strategies for inclusion, as more and more people are exposed to the policies and programs that define the process, all will reap benefits in terms of greater productivity, with the direct result of almost universal increased job satisfaction. Granted, there will be pockets of virulent resistance to change, and some people might leave. But those who stay will exhibit a higher degree of job involvement and organizational commitment with less absenteeism and turnover.

No one said it would be easy, but we have no qualms in saying that it will be worthwhile.

Chapter 5

Designing and Delivering
Sexual Orientation Education
in the Workplace

The single most effective strategy for ensuring full inclusion and maximum productivity where sexual orientation is concerned is a meaningful education program on the subject.

Rather than turning a blind eye to existing challenges in the workplace, either between workers and the organization or between individual employees or groups of employees, or taking the tack that if you ignore it long enough it will all go away (it won't), the best, most cost-effective, and most efficient strategy is to face the issue head-on and deal with it, again through education.

Adults rate corporate-sponsored education programs higher for reliability than any other information source. More than half of the adult employees surveyed would like more, not less, workplace education that delivers more information about what they consider to be difficult issues.[1] Interestingly, the three topics left out of most initial forays into diversity education by corporations are HIV/AIDS and other STD and health-related topics; sexual orientation; and information about people with disabilities. These three are also the ones named most often by people as topics they'd like to see covered in workplace education programs.

These statements might encourage organizations to rush right in and seize the educational day, but they are double-edged swords to be handled carefully. The same adults who say they place high value on information from their employers can also be quite critical about the intent and long-term effects of such education. Employees want more than just good information. They also want the spirit and the methodology to be beyond reproach.

To plan for a program's intent and effectiveness, a company must first understand the difference between workplace education and workplace training. They are not the same, especially when the focus is sexual orientation. Education provides knowledge; training improves skills. Put another way, education provides information about the *what* or *why* of a topic; training deals with the *how*. When the objective is delivery of an effective program about a hypersensitive topic, understanding the difference between education and training (and making sure you are attempting to provide a mixture of both in this discipline) is extremely important.

Applying only strict training methodology to interpersonal relationships robs people of the quality that supposedly separates us from animals in the first place: the ability to think for ourselves and determine our actions on the basis of our thoughts. An effective workplace education program focused on sexual orientation attempts to educate people about concepts such as the inherent nature of sexual orientation, the validity of same-sex-based families, or the rationale for equitable treatment of gays in the workplace or in all places. Acknowledging for the umpteenth time that it is workplace behavior and not beliefs that we want to positively influence, we insist that the only effective strategy is education. The courses we design or recommend include a training aspect in that there is, or should be, a "how to" portion of the program when participants are given the opportunity to apply what they've learned to situations in that workplace.

In our programs we actively encourage our participants to think for themselves, not to automatically accept or reject any information they get in our sessions as absolutely right or wrong from the onset, but to simply acknowledge that much of it is likely new to them and that they should take time to process and completely consider it before they leap to a conclusion. We continually emphasize in our program that whatever we are saying at that moment is being offered for "the participants' consideration" and that they may do with it as they choose. It has been our experience, without doubt, that upon hearing what we bring to these "edusessions," people do take the time to consider new information and they do see the validity in adjusting their behavior—and perhaps sometimes also their attitudes—because of it.

MAKE EDUCATION A PROCESS

We started this chapter by saying that adults rate information they receive from the workplace as more reliable than that from any other source. This is promising because employers therefore enjoy a potential to ensure that the time and money they spend on workplace education brings a positive return on investment; it is simultaneously dangerous because employers bear a responsibility to ensure that positive change does in fact occur. Chances are, an employer that tries to effect change will get only one chance to do it effectively. First impressions are crucial.

When it comes to organizational programs or initiatives, employees take the cynical low road first. If employees believe that a program is being offered because management is bowing to some fad and that the initiatives are not completely supported by solid business reasons or personal conviction on the part of management, the effort will fail. A strategy to overcome this risk is to consider not launching a program at all, but to sell a message that happens to have a program behind it. In other words, *don't develop a finite initiative. Develop a process with never-ending possibilities.*

Step 1. Commit to an open-ended, open-minded process of workplace education.

Step 2. Use a needs assessment tool to determine the tenor of the organization concerning gay people.

Step 3. Pay careful attention to program design; make sure it's the best combination of elements for your organization.

Step 4. Make provisions for continual reinforcement of messages, which lends a "continual full circle" dynamic to the process.

Step 1: Commit to a Process of Workplace Education

Without committed and full support from appropriate management, up to and definitely including the highest echelons of an organization, the process will not only fail, it will never get started. The experience of the diversity manager at a petroleum company, who could speak to us only anonymously, attests to this:

I hope to address sexual orientation at work in our diversity education, but my organization is not willing to deal with this part of diversity in public. Sexual orientation is still that one area of diversity that makes them say, "Well, I'm not going to discriminate against them because they are gay, but I'm not going to value the fact that they are gay either" and of course, that attitude and stance results in discrimination.

We don't have a lot of latitude over what we do at our site. I know we have gay people here who are suffering and that their suffering has a negative impact on our bottom line, but when I told our headquarters group that we wanted to include gay issues, there was no inclination to commit to that education. So all I know is, if I don't get support from our diversity management group, I won't be able to do anything.

Step 2: Use a Needs Assessment Tool

Tweaking organizational thinking to accept education as part of a diversity process—and to include sexual orientation as part of that education—is most easily accomplished by doing a needs assessment. Some call it a "cultural audit" or "cultural evaluation." Needs assessments have a direct relationship to a common management principle: *No solution will be applied to any problem or potential problem until management is sure a problem exists.*

There was a time when Prudential noticed that many of its black employees were leaving the corporation. It directed a survey to that portion of its employee base and a large sampling of the rest of its personnel. Management discovered that a majority of respondents among people of color, women, Asian Americans, and other minority groups felt that management was insensitive to diversity issues. Prudential developed a process of diversity management, including education.

According to Charles Thomas, vice president of human resources, Prudential's diversity effort has gained status as a solid part of the corporate culture since its establishment in the late 1980s. "People are no longer afraid to talk about differences or use the words 'black' or 'white' or 'gay' or 'lesbian' because management examined the core values of the company and installed a process to correct the deficient ones."[2]

Go back to the beginning of any honest diversity effort; you'll find without exception that it started with an assessment of the environment. Whether the assessment is undertaken because human resources management takes the initiative, or whether it is forced on the organization by the activism of a group of employees (which is common in the case of sexual orientation), these assessments are vital to the development of a solid diversity effort. For gay people in the workplace, these assessments can also be the first time management acknowledges their existence at all.

Gay people fall victim to many workplace Catch-22s. One of them is that if they don't stand up, come out, and make their needs known, then those needs most likely won't be addressed. On the other hand, gay people's overall fear of standing up and being counted is the best indication that the organization has a problem in the first place.

One thing that has changed dramatically in the years since our first edition came out is the willingness of gay employees to identify themselves and work to form alliances with other people who are also gay or who for any number of reasons share their commitment to a fully inclusive, fully satisfactory workplace for all. Along with growing visibility on the basis of sexual orientation comes growing visibility on the basis of gender identification. But as good as this increased visibility is, it is obviously not good enough. Take, for example, a statistic from the Ford Motor Company: 10 percent of the membership in Ford GLOBE (Gay, Lesbian, Or Bisexual Employees) comes from production plant/manufacturing facilities, but 90 percent of the reported instances of harassment of gay workers comes from those facilities. What this means is that while gay people in those environments are still unsure or are downright afraid to come out of the closet at work, they are being victimized on the basis of their sexual orientation. Ford's response? The right one. Attack the problem with assessment tools and education program delivery—starting in the plants.

Some might argue that since gay people typically hide at work, finding a large enough representative sample can be difficult. We think this difficulty is totally irrelevant for three reasons. First, the point of collecting the data is to gauge an individual's impression of the environment relative to sexual orientation. A person's response is what matters. If a person has a progay or antigay personal agenda, that will undoubtedly be reflected in his or her answers. The questions are designed to find out the potential or existing trouble spots about which the organization can do something.

Second, the intent of the assessment is to construct an educational program leading to rational thought and a possible change in behavior.

Last, the education itself should be part of a diversity management effort, not an initiative aimed at valuing diversity. They are not the same. Diversity management looks at and tries to improve corporate culture for the sake of the productivity and profitability of the entity. Valuing difference is directed at changing personal bias. When it comes to sexual orientation education in the workplace, changing behavior is the key. If biases are changed, it's a bonus.

Some sample statements from our assessment tool are:

- I have never been acquainted with a gay, bisexual, or transgender person at work.
- If a person made his or her nonheterosexual orientation known to me, I would make every effort to disassociate from him or her even in the context of our work responsibilities.
- Our customers will not do business with us if we have policies that are supportive of gays.
- Extending benefits to gays will bankrupt the company because of HIV.
- Including sexual orientation in our nondiscrimination policy gives special rights to gays.
- If a co-worker "came out" to me, I would not know what to do or say. I'm not even sure I know what "coming out" is.
- I think trust between co-workers is important because_____.
- If someone came out to me, I would counsel him or her to stay in the closet in this environment.

The answers and comments we collect from our assessment tool paint a detailed picture for management as to their work environment relative to sexual orientation. From that, an educational program can be devised.

Step 3: Pay Careful Attention to Program Design

Although we complain about it, most of us do actually use some of the information we learned in high school or college on a fairly regular basis. And there is something to support the notion that formal schooling should last about twelve years if not more. There's a lot to know and you can only cram so much into a single day or year.

The same holds true for workplace education for adults; there are no quick fixes or easy answers to questions that concern any part of the human condition—this may be more true of sexual orientation than of any other aspect of employee diversity nowadays. So, the organization needs to look at these types of programs as a process that is going to require some up-front work, some piloting and continual evaluation to make sure the goals are being met.

We are proponents of a modular approach to this education that is based on an eight-hour course comprising six and a half hours of content in an eight-hour day. This approach is not only comprehensive in its most complete variation, it is easily customized to meet the needs of a given organization and also the needs of subgroups (e.g., management versus line workers) or business units (e.g., engineering versus manufacturing) or other differentiators (e.g., a session in Dallas versus a session in Seattle) that are common to organizations of all sizes and types.

Modularity in development and delivery also aids an organization's efforts to put a committed, open-ended, and open-minded face on its sexual orientation training. Regardless of how well the needs assessment prepares the organization and the facilitators, new insights and unforeseen events can instantaneously put a new spin on the whole process. Modularity allows such bumps and twists to be accounted for seamlessly. It also allows for more content to be added over time and for present content to be continually adjusted to ensure the very best program for that organization.

In general, we typically design and deliver programs that conform to the following broad outline:[3]

- A very good program can be facilitated with three and a half hours of content in a four-hour (or half-day) space. The longer the program, of course, the more time for exercises, personal input from the facilitator and the participants, and more structured discussions.
- It is very important that the course be a structured event with specific objectives and key learning points.

- It is also very important that, regardless of time frame, people feel that they have the ability to express themselves, ask questions, or what have you. It's this part that benefits from professional facilitation. When turned over to trained educators, they must be coached extremely well in all facets of the conversation so that they can handle whatever comes up professionally, responsibly, and with the ability to take care of themselves—regardless of their own orientation—during the program.
- A "workplace issues" portion centers on exercises that bring to bear the ways in which people do—absolutely—bring their personal lives to work all the time and the ways in which not being able to do so can irrevocably damage teamwork relationships.
- A segment about sexual orientation is a "tour" through the dynamics of human sexuality, of which orientation is simply a part. It covers biological sex, gender identity, gender roles, sexual orientation, sexual orientation identity, homophobia, and heterosexism among other things, and it's quite the eye-opener, usually, for participants who never really talked about these topics in that way before.
- Language skills and empathy play a very big part in the work that we do. We believe that a major portion of people's "problem" with sexual orientation, beyond thinking that they don't know or have never met a gay person, is that they honestly don't know what words to use in conversation about the topic. Therefore, a large part of every curriculum we design initially contains content focused on giving people language to discuss their ideas, thoughts, feelings, and so forth about this subject.
- There's an in-depth look at why orientation is a business issue that provides insight to employees on why this all matters to the bottom line.
- How all of the content can be and is applied to that particular workplace is a very important part of the program. It's vital to give people the opportunity to see and to use what they've been offered in real work-world situations and to let them practice—using designed exercises—how it all really plays out at work. Perhaps among the most important of these is an exercise that allows people to put the mantra "behavior, not

beliefs" into solid practice in the safety of this course. It's really quite effective.

- We also put a lot of thought into what the participants get, in the way of printed materials, in conjunction with the course. Typically, a participant's manual is developed and distributed that presents the key points of the course, serves as a workbook for use during the program, and also provides background and additional resource material for the participants to take away with them.[4] Usually this includes the objectives for the course, the core values and business principles driving the course at that organization, key points of course content, specific strategies participants can use to engender change in the workplace (previously described in Chapter 4 as "change agent strategies"), a bibliography (and it's important that this include books that represent all points of view on the topic), a list of additional resources both internal and external to the organization, and, without exception, an evaluation form.

Step 4: Make Provisions for Continual Reinforcement of Messages

Reinforcement has two parts: accountability and constant reevaluation. Accountability is determined in two ways. The first is whether education about sexual orientation is perceived as fully integrated in the overall strategy of the organization. The second is whether the organization identifies a person or persons who are held directly responsible for making sure that initiatives are enforced.

A program on a topic such as this, which has the potential to cause some consternation among members of the workforce, must have a focal point. Typically we've found that there is more consternation before a program is actually offered than afterward; people think that a course of education on sexual orientation is much different than it actually is. It's also been our experience that even the most hearty naysayers get something out of a well-designed course and, at the very least, have no reason to fear what transpires during the course.

Making a single person at each site accountable for the course is very important so that people with positions about the program, either way, can express their comments to a knowledgeable person before and after. All of these comments must be acknowledged in the short term so that it doesn't seem as though the organization is just serving up the "cause du jour."

Constant reevaluation piggybacks off of the accountability efforts. Every session of the program must end with an evaluation form and every evaluation form must be read by the course designers, the facilitators, and the people responsible for the educational initiative at that site and for the organization as a whole. Any diversity program designers or facilitators who think they know everything, even about their own subject area, are bad educators. We constantly learn as we teach our course and we constantly change our course to reflect what we've learned. To do otherwise is unprofessional and irresponsible, and it's bad education. Further, these evaluation forms often kick up strategies for other reinforcement methods at a given site because participants will make recommendations for the kinds of programs or displays that they would like to see or additional information or resources they would like to have.

THREE QUESTIONS

Three questions are common to our work and asked by almost all of our clients sooner or later.

How does the organization ensure that the education effort won't do more harm than good?

We don't believe that education in and of itself ever poses a danger to anyone. But delivered by the wrong people for the wrong reasons and without adequate preparation, education can be devastating to an organization.

One diversity director we know, who requested anonymity, learned this lesson the very hard way. A particular employee in her company who happened to be gay was also disliked by a number of his colleagues. Being gay was acknowledged as one of the reasons he was disliked, but it was not the only reason. Being gay was, however, the aspect of this individual targeted by those who did not like him. Their gay-bashing and harassment were blatantly discriminatory and obnoxious both to the employee and to management.

Acting in good faith, appropriate company representatives first spoke to each of the harassing employees individually and told them that continued abuse of the individual for any reason would not be tolerated. Then management attempted to clear the air by sitting all the parties down and allowing them to express themselves. This turned out to be a major mistake. The director said,

> In trying to educate these employees in this situation, we actually made things worse because we allowed peple to express themselves and a lot of what they had to say could only be described as vehemently interpersonally homophobic. We were not prepared to address their homophobia in any constructive way at that time, and the employee who was being harassed suffered further by finding out how pointed and hateful the attitudes of his coworkers were about him.

Does the facilitator of sexual orientation education have to be gay?

When we first wrote this book we said that, "the short answer is no, the longer answer is it wouldn't hurt, and the best answer is yes." We now adjust this answer to be simply, "no."

The reason for this change of heart, if you wish to call it that, is that education on the topic of sexual orientation is about just that: sexual orientation, and everyone has one. The most important characteristic of a facilitator is not being nonheterosexual; the most important characteristic is being completely knowledgeable and prepared about the subject, over and above what the facilitator will actually teach. People ask some interesting questions and raise some interesting points for discussion. A well-rounded understanding of the topic is what's called for, not status for gays as "a minority."

We have witnessed some of the best facilitation of programs we've helped develop by heterosexual facilitators. The reason these people were so effective was that they worked hard to find ways to relate experiences in their lives to the course material. Since the majority of their participants were also heterosexual, the bridges these people built by example were strong and powerfully affecting.

We will say, however, that it is also enormously helpful if one or both facilitators (in team teaching situations, for which we do advocate in training the educator models) happen not to be nonheterosexual, to have a member of the workforce step up and talk about what it's like to be gay or bi or transgender there. Again, this is an area where the employee alliance can make a significant contribution by having an internal "speaker's bureau." If no such resource is in place at the organization, speaker's bureaus and other organizations typically exist in metropolitan areas who can lend some support in a given location that doesn't have its own.

Should sexual orientation education be mandatory?

As we reported in the first edition, Rynes and Rosen in their study of workplace diversity education concluded that it should be mandatory for all.[5] We respectfully disagreed then and we still do. Our opinion is that these programs should be mandatory for senior management (however that term is defined by the organization) because these are people with an obligation to focus on behavior, not beliefs, in the workplace. However, courses should not be mandatory—although freely recommended and attendance encouraged and certainly not blocked—for everyone else.

These arguments go back to the data that indicate a strong desire for these kinds of programs at work in the first place. If you build them, and build them right, people will come . . . of their own accord.

THE IMPLEMENTATION
OF SEXUAL ORIENTATION EDUCATION

An implementation scheme will, in overview, consist of the following elements:

- Awareness raising and buy-in
- Piloting
- Rollout

Awareness Raising and Buy-In

The process begins with awareness raising, typically at the most senior level of the organization, and to the senior-level staff's direct reports who will be charged with implementation of the eventual, detailed plan.

When dealing with people at the highest levels, two things are most important: respect for time and directness. Our experience is that the best results come when members of senior management are presented with the content targeted for their organization and the general scope of the delivery plan on a long-term basis. It's extremely important that these people:

- raise their own awareness level about the subject of sexual orientation in their workplace so that they can make decisions about it; and
- have an opportunity in comfortable surroundings and with their peers to discuss their own feelings and get their questions answered so that they can act in concert with their professional responsibilities while leaving their beliefs intact.

To fulfill these goals, we usually design a program that is more presentation, less workshop (although we do include some exercise elements when we can) in conjunction with the implementers at the organization, i.e., people who are typically charged with curriculum design and who usually bring such matters to the attention of senior management.

If the job is done correctly, the design/implementation team leaves with a mandate to develop a program for general dissemination to the organization and instructions to map out exactly what that will look like, how long it will take, and what it will cost. Tacit approval is typically also given for those who have job responsibility for these programs to proceed, and usually a member of senior management is assigned to keep tabs on the rollout over the next weeks, months, and years.

This last is very important. It speaks to the accountability factor that we discussed previously. A member of senior management must be charged with knowing the status of this program. This person needs to be kept informed via status reports, should get copies of all of the evaluations from every session of the course, and should have some visible way for employees to communicate with him or her if lower echelons of feedback cannot adequately address a question or a concern.

Piloting

The piloting of the program should be as extensive as possible and calls into play the constant reevaluation of the course prior to the generation of "final materials" for it. With the caveat we raised before that the course is never "finished," materials can likely be generated that would serve well through its life span at the organization.

If the organization has, for example, six levels of management that operate in four distinct kinds of facilities in every geographic region of the United States and Canada, then every attempt should be made to pilot the course to as many different combinations of these as possible. We have not rolled out a long-term program based on less than a dozen pilots, nor would we recommend it.

This number of pilots allows for optimum feedback, and, of course, the people who undergo them also get the benefit of the education. We also highly recommend that pilots go to what we call "worst-first" facilities. In other words, if the organization has had one or more incidents at a particular facility related to sexual orientation in the workplace, pilot the program there first, or certainly include it in the pilot phase.

This accomplishes two things: first, it sends a message that the organization acknowledges that a challenge exists and it means to face it head on and resolve it to the best of its ability; second, the feedback engendered from such locations is extremely valuable because you get a sense of the extremes at work in your organization living in concert with the moderates. Don't shy away from these places; go there first and learn. What you learn will help build a better course faster.

Once through the pilot process, you may find it advisable to go back, especially to the "worst-first" sites, and offer the finished course again. Encourage people who attended the pilot to come back. They will see that their input has been incorporated, which will send another positive message that the organization is listening and acting upon what it hears.

Beyond addressing the hot spots in terms of place, the piloting process allows you to address the hot spots in terms of content. We cannot count the number of managers, directors, and higher executives in human resources who would rather not deal with this topic because it is perceived as too tough to tackle. It is tough, but not impossible, and it is completely worthwhile. Piloting the program allows people at all levels and from all job functions to accept the truth of these statements.

Another benefit of extensive piloting is identifying people in the organization who, down the road, might make good facilitators of the program. It has been our experience that piloting, because it is so focused on feedback and getting people to think about what they are learning, causes many to fully incorporate the materials in ways that encourage their interest in teaching it. It's good to meet these people face-to-face to evaluate their reasons and their interest in facilitating the course while you are evaluating the course as a whole. When you're ready for full rollout and perhaps a train-the-trainer aspect, what you've learned about people will prove as valuable as what you've learned about the material.

But again, the primary reason to pilot as much as possible is to make the content optimal for your organization.

Rollout

It's in the rollout phase that the true meaning of commitment is defined for an organization. It's here that you learn if you're in for the long haul, because a long haul it will be. Rollout plans must call for the most efficient and cost-effective ways to make the education as widely available as possible to the broadest number of employees conceivable. A typical model will have these elements:

- A definition of "management" is arrived at for an organization across functions, facilities, and geographies, and managers will typically participate in sessions of the program facilitated by a professional who had a hand in the development and design of the program.
- In conjunction with the hands-on education of management, appropriate, suitable, qualified, and interested members of the employee population will be identified who can deliver the program after receiving extensive training. These people may come from human resources, diversity, the alliance, from organizational development (OD), or, as noted previously, making themselves known during the piloting of the program.
- A number of people will be selected to undergo a "boot camp" of sorts to prepare them to teach the course. We recommend that:

—At least twice the number of people projected to be necessary to facilitate the course to X number of people over Y time period be invited, because some of them won't come and some will be dropped as inappropriate, either by the core facilitator or voluntarily. This attrition rate is historically half of the original pool.

—The educators are trained to work in teams. There is a lot to know; these people are not professional facilitators (though some are) and are not typically experts on the subject of sexual orientation (although they'll be close after the boot camp). Working in teams of two seems to be the best model.

—The boot camp should be absolutely no less than five full working days; eight is optimum.

• Once the educators have been trained, they begin to facilitate the course for audiences of management, supervisors, salaried workers, union workers, line employees, and mixtures thereof with the professional facilitator—at least a half-dozen cofacilitated sessions per team for organizations of 5,000 or more. (*Note:* these numbers are, obviously, adjusted by size and scope of the organization as is the number, for example, of teams trained to educate.)

• Finally, the teams deliver the programs themselves, with or without the professional facilitator present strictly to observe and offer feedback to help with continuous improvement of the teams.

Depending on size, organizations sometimes prefer that the entire rollout be handled and delivered by professional facilitators, but we see no reason why excellent programs cannot be delivered by trained staff at an organization, especially in those cases where the trained educators are, by profession, facilitators of workplace education.

As you can see, quite a commitment of time, energy, money, and resources is implied by this plan. But the results of such effort, in dollars, commonly work out to be less than $100 per employee who undergoes a half-day program when these programs are offered per this model to 2,500 to 5,000 employees over an eighteen-month period. And the longer you allow the program to continue, the more people are exposed to the education at an even lower per-person cost.

ADJUNCT DISCUSSIONS:
HIV/AIDS EDUCATION
AND MARKET ACQUISITION EDUCATION

When *Straight Talk* was first published, there was an undeniable and extremely unfortunate connection in the minds of too many people between the word *gay* and the acronym AIDS. Thankfully, that connection is not so definite anymore; unfortunately, transmission of HIV and other sexually transmitted diseases (STDs) has not abated and in some cases is on the increase in the United States and elsewhere among all people regardless of sexual orientation, gender identification, income level, race, age, or any other factor you might care to throw in. Therefore, informational programs on these topics are of enormous value and should be considered.

We made a conscious choice to capitalize on this progress, now that people no longer automatically say "AIDS" right after "gay," in that no chapter in this edition is devoted to HIV/AIDS education or policy in the workplace. However, we would like to make the following points in recognition of the fact that this is a considerable and very legitimate ongoing health concern all over the world.

HIV/AIDS and STDs in the Workplace—
Some Useful Information

Today in the United States, one in seventy-five men is currently infected.[6] AIDS is the second leading cause of death for men ages eighteen to forty-four. One in 600 women is currently infected. AIDS is the third leading cause of death for women ages twenty-five to forty-four as of 1997. In a few years, AIDS will be the second leading cause of death for women in this age group. And it is eight times easier for a woman to become infected than for a man who has sex with women.

The fastest growing group of people labeled as having AIDS are women; they now account for 20 percent of newly reported AIDS cases. Youths are the second fastest growing group of people with AIDS; twenty-five a day become infected.

AIDS is already the fifth leading cause of death for youths ages fifteen to twenty-four. One study found that more than 1 in 300 college students is infected. Over half of all cases of AIDS are among youths twenty-five and younger.

Sexually transmitted diseases are an epidemic among teens. AIDS, too, is a sexually transmitted disease. Other STDs include chlamydia, gonorrhea, herpes, and syphilis. Teens account for over 25 percent of all cases of STDs. And STDs make it easier for the AIDS virus to pass from one person to another by damaging cells through which the virus can enter the blood system.

Most of the same behaviors that protect against STDs also protect against HIV infection. However, teens are engaging in the kinds of high-risk behaviors that spread AIDS and other STDs. Twenty-seven percent of sexually active teens (ages fifteen to nineteen) have had thirty or more sexual partners; 11 percent frequently engage in anal intercourse, and 25 percent have used the services of a sex worker.

How many teens are having sex? *Answer:* 70 percent. How many teens know that you can become infected with AIDS through sexual activity? *Answer:* over 90 percent. How many teens think they are going to become infected through sex? *Answer:* less than 10 percent. This is like ten kids joining hands and jumping from a fifty-story building. Each one is thinking that only the other nine are going to be killed. To save their lives, we must educate young people about AIDS. And AIDS education does work, even with teenagers.

AIDS is really a worldwide pandemic. Pandemic means that it is an epidemic that is widespread over a large region or regions. In fact, every country in the world has reported cases of AIDS, for a total of 35 million. And this number is significantly underreported. One estimate is that by the end of the year 2000 between 50 and 100 million people will be infected with the virus that causes AIDS. This pandemic is going to impoverish millions of families, create thousands of orphans, cause social and political unrest, reverse the economic and social gains made by developing countries, destabilize governments, and severely affect businesses, including U.S. global and domestic businesses.

AIDS is a business issue. It is a business issue because AIDS will affect the workplace and because AIDS is in the workplace. Ninety percent of people with AIDS are in the workplace. AIDS is a business issue because it affects our co-workers who have AIDS or who are the parent, child, aunt, uncle, brother or sister, husband, wife, or partner of someone with AIDS.

Two out of every three large businesses and nearly one out of ten smaller businesses are aware that they have employees with AIDS in their workplaces. Sooner or later every workplace will be impacted by AIDS.

Seventy-five percent of people want AIDS education, and their most trusted source of AIDS education is the workplace.

More people in the workplace are affected by AIDS than we realize. Approximately 1 in 100 workers is infected with the AIDS virus, and this number is still growing. Other employees are also affected by AIDS. Three in 100 people are caregivers for someone with AIDS or who is infected with HIV. These are the spouses or domestic partners, brothers or sisters, parents, grandparents, friends, and neighbors. These people are almost as hidden as people with AIDS. They too are affected by discrimination and fear and often prefer not to tell others that a person with AIDS is in their lives.

Ten in 100 people are the "worried well." These are people who have engaged in high-risk behaviors and are worried that they may be infected.

At least 30 in 100 people are fearful and misinformed about AIDS. These are people who believe that AIDS can be "caught" just by working alongside someone with AIDS or touching something that a person with AIDS has touched, or using the same bathroom or shower as a person with AIDS. This kind of fear can lead to unnecessary problems in the workplace. You cannot "catch" AIDS from casual contact in the workplace, but people need to be educated about AIDS in order to respond sensibly to AIDS in the workplace.

There are really three epidemics: One is AIDS. The second epidemic is fear and denial. One government survey shows that people know less about AIDS today than they did five years ago. In many ways, it is ignorance that is spreading this disease. The third epidemic is discrimination and harassment. This is the hidden epidemic, which is even more infectious than AIDS. Even today people with AIDS lose their jobs, are denied health care, and are abandoned by their families. Discrimination and harassment begin with misinformation and are spread through fear. We can stop all three epidemics.

Every worker in the United States has a right to a safe work environment. HIV disease is not airborne; it is a blood-borne disease and is spread primarily through sex and sharing injection needles. According to the U.S. Surgeon General, "HIV is not spread through common everyday contact," such as in most workplaces.

The Americans with Disabilities Act, known as the ADA, made HIV disease a protected disability, like blindness, deafness, or other physical handicaps. The law prohibits discrimination against people with HIV disease in hiring, employment, or termination. The law also covers people who are perceived to have HIV disease, such as a family member or a caregiver of a person with HIV disease. In general, an individual cannot be refused employment or terminated solely on the basis that the person has or is perceived to have HIV disease. Discrimination is also prohibited in recruitment, promotion, training, layoffs, compensation, job assignments, leaves of absence, and benefits.

Ninety percent of people with HIV disease are in the workplace. Most want to continue to work. In most cases, simple accommodations mean that they can go on working. Research shows that two key factors influencing whether people with HIV continue to work are control of the pace of work and control of the scheduling. People with HIV disease tend to leave the workplace if they cannot control these two factors. Those who can control them tend to stay in the workplace.

All of us value our privacy. Most of us feel our finances and health records are private. We might tell others about our health issues, but we feel that our privacy has been invaded if others tell people about our health issues without our permission. This is true for people with HIV disease as much as it is for anyone else.

Medical information is legally considered private. This means that no one is to reveal medical information without the individual's permission. If a co-worker tells you about his or her health condition, find out whether it is all right for you to tell others. The rule of thumb for HIV disease is: if you are told by a co-worker that he or she has HIV disease, do not repeat this information without the express permission of the individual. This is also true for supervisors; you may not tell anyone without the individual's permission. You can, however, seek and use resources by describing the general situation and not identifying the individual person.

Many companies require a physical examination before an individual is hired. This examination is intended to determine whether the individual is fit to do the job for which he or she is being hired. It is not intended to determine the individual's general state of health. People are routinely hired who have preexisting health problems, such as cancer, when these problems do not inhibit their ability to do the job. Guided by this principle, people with HIV disease are hired when they are fit to do the job in question, although reasonable accommodations are made in some cases.

In many states it is against the law to require an individual to take an HIV antibody test without his or her voluntary consent. It is against the law to disclose HIV antibody test results without the individual's voluntary consent. The results are medical information which is protected by privacy law.

HIV disease is treated like all other serious health conditions. Just as people with heart disease or cancer have medical insurance, sick leave, and disability insurance, so do people with HIV disease. The ADA makes it illegal to discriminate against people in the provision of benefits solely on the basis of HIV disease.

When we think of HIV disease in the workplace, we usually think of the employee with HIV disease. But HIV affects more than the person with the disease; it affects employees who are caregivers for someone with HIV, the supervisors of employees with HIV, caregivers, and co-workers, as well.

It is not unusual for co-workers and supervisors to have mixed feelings about working with an employee with HIV disease. We all have a kind of built-in fear of disease, particularly one as serious as HIV. On the other hand, we feel sympathetic and want to support a co-worker with an illness. Usually these co-workers are not strangers; they are people with whom we have worked and are friendly.

Co-workers may have mixed feelings about an employee who is a caregiver for someone with HIV disease. Some will ask, "Can you catch HIV from a caregiver?" The simple answer is no, but this demonstrates the need for AIDS education so that people can learn the facts.

On the other hand, people may be concerned that a co-worker with HIV disease might catch something from them, such as a cold or flu, because of the co-worker's weakened immune system. Surprisingly, people whose immune systems are impaired by HIV disease are not more susceptible to colds and flu. HIV is very selective in its immune system damage. People with HIV disease are not especially vulnerable to these ordinary microorganisms and viruses.

Employees with HIV disease and caregivers, too, may have mixed emotions. Employees with HIV may be fearful of co-workers' responses—anger, fear, rejection, or harassment. But they also want to avoid feeling isolated and cut off from the friendship and support of their co-workers. This is true for caregivers, as well. We can help by getting educated about HIV disease and making it clear that we support people affected by the disease.

In the workplace, who is the first person an employee with HIV disease tells? *Answer:* a co-worker. Who is the second person? *Answer:* his or her supervisor. How do you respond? We may feel that we don't know the "right" thing to say when someone says he or she has HIV disease. Respond with your heart: "How are you doing?" or "How can I help?" Think how you would want to be treated if you were in a similar situation.

Also, respect the person's privacy. Do not tell others about your co-worker's condition without his or her permission. Realize the limits of your role. If you are a supervisor, your role is the management of performance. If you are a co-worker, make sure the person knows what resources are available to him or her.

Acknowledge your own feelings—possibly your mixed emotions. If you are fearful, get more education about HIV disease. Resources— management, educational, legal, and so on—are available to you too; use them.

For employees with HIV disease and for caregivers: acknowledge your own mixed emotions. Talk out your concerns and questions with friends, family, or other resources. Consider the advantages, as well as the possible disadvantages, of informing your supervisor and co-workers that you have HIV disease or that you are a caregiver. It takes a lot of effort to "hide," which may impair your health. Help create or maintain a work environment that is supportive of people affected by HIV disease. Educate others about HIV disease and encourage AIDS education.

Finally, know and use resources are available to you both in your workplace and in the community.

Gay Market Acquisition Education:
An Idea Whose Time Is Here

Another adjunct education program that organizations might consider is bringing certain parts of their staff "up to speed" on the gay market for the purpose of directing their marketing and sales efforts to it. This would consist of deconstructing sexual orientation to the level and for the purposes of understanding how a person's sexual orientation (especially if not in the majority) affects that person's decisions relative to products and services.

For example, if a petroleum company wanted to appeal to this market, could they produce something called "Gay Gas"? If a company that makes products for babies wanted to capitalize on what is being referred to as the "Gayby Boom," could there be a market for gay diapers or gay formula? On one hand, such suggestions are preposterous, but on the other, they are not. As discussed before, marketing to a constituency sometimes involves nothing more than showing those people in advertising imagery.

Where the gay market might intersect with this theory is in organizations understanding what particular needs gay people have in American society, for example, due to the existence of relationships that are real but that are not legal. The provisions gay people have to make to protect our families legally and fiscally, to name just two, are considerable. We cannot play by the same rules as the heterosexual majority because we aren't allowed to. More about what that means to the individual and to businesses as those rules change—and they are changing—is covered in some detail in Chapter 7. But for now the question is, is there an element of education that can be focused on acquisition of a market that has these special needs? We believe the answer is yes.

Organizations can and should be looking at the following questions:

- What is orientation?
- What does one's orientation mean in terms of one's life decisions?
- How are aspects of finances and legality affected by sexual orientation?
- How are aspects of various common and ordinary services and products affected by sexual orientation?

- Are there characteristics particular to people of a nonheterosexual orientation that make them viable customers for this organization?
- Does the necessity for people of a nonheterosexual orientation or minority gender identification to continually "think outside the box" make them viable candidates for our products and services?
- In what ways could we adjust current marketing and sales strategies to specifically target this potential market?
- What new strategies can we come up with to target them, and what do our people need to know about nonheterosexual people in order to leverage these strategies to their fullest?

Based on the answers to these and more questions that would need be asked, a curriculum for internal sales and marketing training can be developed. What we are talking about here is obviously a targeted marketing scheme, but with a twist. Utilizing principles of diversity education, the organization can be not only proactive or reactive in dealing with internal workplace situations founded in sexual orientation, it can be proactive in leveraging the diversity program to create a new market niche if its products, services, or mission lends itself to it. We can think of hundreds of business types—from auto makers to financial services companies to law firms to banks to, well, the list is endless indeed—that could.

Chapter 6

The Ins and Outs
of Domestic Partner Benefits

In 1995, fewer than 300 organizations in the United States offered domestic partner benefits, also called partner benefits or
DPBs, to the same-sex and, in some cases, opposite-sex partners of
their employees.[1] At the turn of the twenty-first century, the confirmed number of organizations who offer these benefits is well
over 3,500. The real number (albeit unconfirmed) is probably over
5,000. And while the 300 or so organizations who offered them
back in the mid-1990s tended to be only in high-tech, law, entertainment, or private institutions of higher education, today's list represents everything from Fortune 10 companies to the smallest retail
outfits in America.

We don't include a list of the confirmed organizations in our
books because it would be obsolete the day after we wrote it. Two to
three employers per week are adding these benefits; only four employers have reneged on them since 1982 (Perot Systems, Storage-
Tek, the City of Boston, and ExxonMobil), and two-thirds of the
3,500 that we've confirmed offer the benefits to opposite-sex couples along with same-sex couples and their children.

Why the explosion in DPBs? Two simple reasons. First, according to the U.S. Census Bureau in 1994 and 1998, the number of
Americans living in unmarried-partner households increased at five
times the rate of married-couple households. In 1998, 5.9 million
people in the United States were living with a partner. Of these,
approximately 28 percent, or 1.7 million people, were in same-sex
relationships.[2]

The second reason is, as Mr. Clinton's campaign stated so elo-
quently in 1992, "It's the economy, stupid." For example, to aug-

ment all we've said before about economics driving increased inclusion, according to the *Denver Post,* companies are improving their benefits packages to hold on to valuable part-time workers in the tight labor market.[3] Human resources managers who were polled by RewardsPlus.com, a Web-based benefits services firm, found that one-third of companies with 1,000 or more part-time workers are giving these part-timers medical benefits. The survey found that 75 percent of employers offer benefits to people who work at least thirty hours per week; 62 percent give them to workers at twenty to twenty-nine hours per week; and 25 percent offer benefits to those working fewer than twenty hours per week.

Benefits to part-time employees are a lot more expensive (due to sheer numbers of eligible persons) than are DPBs. And consider this: The Society of Human Resources Management found in a survey of 279 human resources professionals representing nineteen industries in the United States that DPBs are the number one recruitment tool for executives and the third-ranked recruitment tool for management and line workers.[4] DPBs were found to be a more effective hiring incentive than telecommuting options, hiring bonuses, stock options, and 401K plans, among other things.

All of this is true because people have families—all kinds of families constructed in all kinds of ways—and organizations who are not up to date are losing out today and will continue to lose out tomorrow. As we'll see in Chapter 7, which covers same-sex marriage or legal partnership as concerns business and employment, what's driving these things is more than just desire. What's driving DPBs is the undeniable necessity to keep pace with reality.

THE HISTORY OF WORKPLACE BENEFITS

This working generation (anyone from fifteen to seventy years of age) tends to think of employer-provided benefits as a birthright. They aren't, of course, but they may be the closest most people ever get. Benefits as a form of workplace compensation started in the 1940s, when companies who wanted to pay certain employees more were prohibited by law from doing so by way of simple pay increases. So instead of giving the cash directly to the employee, the employer paid for certain products and services such as insurance or housing on the employee's behalf. For laborers traditionally holding the shorter end of the compensatory stick, workplace benefits derived in part from President Franklin D. Roosevelt's New Deal as a way to subsidize both businesses and employees during and immediately after the Depression.

Since the 1940s, workplace benefits have continued to constitute an integral part of compensation. Even during the boom (no pun intended) years of World War II through the development of the suburbs in the 1950s and 1960s, benefits from the workplace were taken for granted. Employers found new and different ways to package benefits, both for the good of employees and to enhance the attractiveness of their workplace over that of their competitors. Therefore, the idea of benefits constituting a competitive advantage is not a new one. Organizations have been trying to outdo one another in this fashion for decades.

The economic and symbolic importance of workplace benefits is undeniable. The U.S. Chamber of Commerce released a study stating that between 37 and 40 percent of total employee compensation is made up of workplace benefits.[5] In concert with this data, 67 percent of respondents to an Employee Benefit Research survey said they would not give up *any portion* of their employer-provided benefits even in lieu of a higher cash salary.[6] Ironically, the principle that led in part to the creation of such benefits fifty-odd years ago—namely, giving employees benefits in lieu of additional cash salary—is the same one that won't allow employers to back away from this expense now.

These statistics speak to the necessity of providing benefits as a way to attract and maintain labor, and the popularity of DPBs in particular in achieving this goal. When organizations consider the expense as opposed to the return on investment, DPBs are a good bet. This is not to say that all sorts of organizations are not looking for ways to mitigate the expenses relative to employee benefits, because they most certainly are. It is only to say that whatever schemes they come up with, from this point forward, partners regardless of orientation or gender and their dependents will be included.

Some Precedent Setting

In 1997, the City and County of San Francisco mandated DPBs for all partnered employees (regardless of gender or orientation) and their partners from any organization that does business with the City or County. The City estimates that some 12,000 firms in the Bay Area will eventually be affected by this ordinance.

At the end of 1999, Seattle, Los Angeles, and Broward County in Florida followed suit with similar ordinances. While Seattle's is the closest to San Francisco's in scope, Los Angeles and Broward County have taken giant steps in recognizing the needs and familial realities of all of their employees. Also, the State of New York Appeals Court upheld the City of New York's domestic partner laws, which provide for benefits among other things, as have courts finding in favor of these laws in San Francisco, Chicago, and Atlanta.

EQUAL PAY FOR EQUAL WORK

"Domestic partner" or just "partner" has fast become the most popular way for gay people to describe their relationships to their significant others because words such as *spouse* are too intrinsically tied to the legally recognized relationship of marriage. This of course is currently subject to change. Equitable benefits are of vital consequence to gay employees because they represent both recognition of gay relationships and, perhaps more important, they signify equal pay for equal work. In awarding DPBs, the employer is not granting a "new" or "special" benefit to its unmarried, partnered employees. Existing benefits are merely extended to another classification of employee, based on an expanded set of criteria for eligibility. This causes fluctuation of out-of-pocket costs, while soft benefits, which clearly cost the organization something, have a cost thought to be more intangible. In some industries, retail being one, the line between strictly hard and soft benefits can be blurred by certain questions, such as employee discounts on products. Hard benefits are typically thought of as the cost-intensive benefits such as medical, dental, and pension benefits. Soft benefits are less cost intensive (or are at least thought of as such) and include benefits such as bereavement leave, use of company facilities, relocation assistance, and so forth.

The reason for this is that, as we will examine in much more detail under The Cost section of Domestic Partner Benefits in this chapter, hard benefits typically have an imputable (taxable) value to the employee due to the nonlegal status of that person's relationship with his or her partner and/or the partner's children.

Examples of soft benefits include the following:

- Private sector: bereavement leave, sick leave, parenting leave, employee discounts, health and fitness programs, relocation benefits
- Public sector: access to school records, registration of partnership, visitation rights in hospitals or prisons, and tax benefits for companies in the cities that recognize domestic partners
- College and university: child care, faculty/staff privileges, student/faculty housing, university ID privileges, tuition waiver or reimbursement

The number of organizations in the United States with full benefits (read: hard benefits) is much lower than the number of those with some type of soft benefits for (usually) same-sex partners. Due to the frequency with which such soft benefits are offered without organizational stipulation or documentation, it remains impossible to gauge how many organizations today are offering some form of soft benefits to their employees and their partners. And, for the record, we don't consider (nor do most others) organizations that offer only soft benefits as having partner benefits.

Examples of hard benefits (regardless of market sector) include:

- Medical/Dental
- Pension
- Insurance

Any and all benefits that are offered to legal spouses and dependents of employees can, and probably should, be offered to partners within the confines of the applicable tax codes.

For example, if the organization provides COBRA and FMLA benefits to families, they should also be extended to partners and their dependent children. If the organization pays the proceeds of a private pension plan to legal spouses, but not to dependents, it should make a provision that such benefits would be paid to partners as well. In the case of private pensions, however, the organization under ERISA regulations is under no obligation to make these payments in the event of the untimely death of the employee.

As far as life insurance is concerned, the organization can allow employees' partners to purchase both life and accidental death/dismemberment insurance through the company if spouses have this option, but there is a tax ramification for this purchase and a tax attorney should be consulted.

In terms of soft benefits, every effort should be made to pointedly include partners, in writing and as a matter of company policy, so that there is no uncertainty on the part of any manager or employee as to whether a gay man may, for example, take a day off to attend the funeral of his partner's father. It is very important that there be no ambiguity in company policy about such matters.

Further, if relocation assistance is provided case by case, as it is in many organizations, whether such assistance is available for partners should also be spelled out.

Should the organization wish to make employee discounts available to partners, it will have to develop a method to track the discounts, due to the tax liability involved.

Medical/Dental Benefits

Although there are no restrictions on partner benefits plans in most jurisdictions, and although most if not all of the standard insurers and HMO/PPO plans write them as standard operating procedures now, some companies still are not writing them either because they choose not to, or they have not yet been asked to, or because they simply have not completed the filings necessary to offer them in all the states where they do business. In the last five years a startling thing has occurred: it is now harder to find an insurance provider who *won't* write these benefits than to find those who will.

There is only one jurisdiction left (Virginia, as of January 2000) in which insurance regulations preclude standard insurers from writing these plans. These rules almost never apply to HMOs/PPOs and they never apply at all to self-insured plans. There are always ways to work around this situation, either by limiting the kinds of plans offered in a place such as Virginia or where some of the organization's providers have declined to participate, or by licensing the plan in another state where the business operates.

Pension Plans

The employer will pay the vested portion of a deceased employee's pension to a legal spouse. It can, if it chooses, also pay any vested monies to a partner. However, under ERISA, if the pension is fully company funded, it need not pay these benefits to the surviving partner.

In the case of a 401K plan, the employee can name as beneficiary any person with an "insurable interest." This is not affected in any way by the implementation of a DPB plan.

Either the employee/retiree or the partner would claim the pension payments as income for tax purposes unless the plan has a tax-qualified status. There is no imputed calculation for the employer either way.

Term Life Insurance

Although employees can buy term life insurance for their spouses, they cannot for partners. A nonlegal spouse cannot be party to group life insurance unless the employee pays the entire premium, due to the tax status of insurance premiums (life and disability).

A partner or any person who can show an insurable interest can, of course, be the beneficiary of a life insurance policy of his or her partner. The proceeds of such policies are taxed as income (depending on estate maneuvers, etc.) and are not the calculation responsibility of the employer.

Employee Stock Ownership

If the corporation allows vested stock to become the property of a legal spouse in the case of death of the employee, then it has the option (as with pensions above) to award that stock to a domestic partner.

Disability Plans

All employees, regardless of family type or marital status, have equal access to the benefits of long- and/or short-term disability insurance. Legal spouses or legal dependents have no additional rights or access under these plans. So, they would not likely apply to a DPB plan.

Adoption Assistance

The following states or districts specifically allow joint adoptions by lesbian and gay couples: Massachusetts, New Jersey, New York, Vermont, and the District of Columbia. (California is mulling a change in status.) Two states specifically do not allow joint adoptions by lesbian and gay couples: Florida and New Hampshire.

Courts in the following states have allowed joint adoptions by lesbian and gay couples (these decisions do not apply statewide): Alabama, Alaska, California, Connecticut, Illinois, Indiana, Maryland, Michigan, Minnesota, Nevada, Oregon, Pennsylvania, Rhode Island, Texas, and Washington.

In all other states, gay and lesbian couples adopt through single-parent, and then second-parent, adoptions. As adoption is an option for a domestic partnership (including nonmarried heterosexuals through single-parent/second-parent adoptions), adoption assistance would likely apply. There is likely an imputed value to monies provided for this purpose similar to that in relocation assistance plans. This tax burden is shared by any employee who accepts such monetary assistance regardless of marital status. However, there may be tax breaks for people who adopt (again regardless of gender, orientation, or marital status); either way, the monies should be treated as taxable income to the employee.

Dependent Care Referral

Because dependant care referral is a service available to "families" and has no imputed/cash value, there would seem to be no reason why it could not be accessed by or for partners and nondependent children of the employee.

Health Care and Dependent Care Spending Accounts

Dependent care expenses are designed to be deducted pretax both to help the employee put money aside for dependent care and to do so while reducing the income tax burden. However, due to the federal tax code, benefits for persons who are not the legal spouse or legal dependent of an employee cannot be deducted pretax. Therefore, there is no benefit for an employee with a nonlegal spouse or nonlegal dependent to provide for those persons in that manner. A private investment plan (or second-parent adoption) might be a more advantageous arrangement.

The organization does have the option to make the plan available in its DPB plans on an after-tax basis and let employees calculate what option is to their fiscal advantage.

Education Assistance for Children

If the corporation's policy calls for education assistance to be provided only to legal dependents, then the employee's nonlegal dependent children (i.e., Does the employee provide for 51 percent of the minor's care and claim the minor as a deduction for tax purposes?) would not qualify for such assistance. The corporation has an option to change the qualifying requirements for such assistance. The value of such assistance would be imputed income unless other tax qualifying events supersede. Please consult a tax advisor for the status of funds for education.

Employee Discounts

Employee discounts have an imputed value that require a separate tracking system, and no elegant solution currently exists (as of January 2000). These discounts are typically not being offered in (retail) DPB plans right now.

Bereavement Leave

Bereavemnet leave is a soft benefit that should be awarded to employees, regardless of gender or orientation, so that they can observe the passing of a loved one. The loved one technically may not be a member of an employee's family (by marriage) but in reality is a member of the family due to the partner relationship. This benefit has no monetary value. It could and should be awarded in the same manner that employees are enabled to attend to family/in-law matters in cases of marital family relationships and responsibilities.

FMLA-Like Leaves and COBRA-Like Arrangements

FMLA, which provides for an employee's leave of absence to care for a family member, and COBRA, which provides for the continuation of medical coverage for a set period after a person leaves his or her job, can both be provided to domestic partners. While the federal acts that initiate these plans do not specifically include nonlegal spouses or dependents, they do not exclude them either (for nonfederal employees outside the auspices of the Office of Personnel Management). Therefore, most organizations with DPB plans make FMLA-like arrangements with employees who are not married or whose dependents are not legal to allow unpaid leave for a twelve-month period with the assurance of job retention, and so forth. And most, if not all, also extend COBRA-like benefits to partners of employees who qualify for COBRA upon discontinuation of their employment.

Neither of these has an imputed value. FMLA benefits do not affect income (except possibly to reduce taxable income when elected), and COBRA requires the payment of premiums in their entirety by the employee/partner with no monetary contribution from the employer after separation.

Employee Assistance Programs

In most employee assistance programs (EAP), it is left to the discretion of the employee to define "family" as he or she sees fit. Because the purpose of an EAP is to provide support to an employee who may have problems involving family, it is usually deemed proper and necessary that the employee be able to assess those individuals who positively or negatively affect his or her life and/or job performance. Therefore, partners are well advised to be included in that group with access to the EAP suite of services.

Relocation Benefits

It is unreasonable of an employer to acknowledge sexual orientation and DPBs without including equitable relocation policies for partners. In almost all cases in the private sector where relocation expenses are reimbursed for spouses, they are also reimbursed for partners (including house-hunting trips, etc.). The value of such assistance would be imputed income unless other tax qualifying events supersede. Please consult a tax advisor for the status of monies for relocation.

THE COST OF DOMESTIC PARTNER BENEFITS

Three questions most often arise during any discussion of DPBs:

- How many people will elect the benefits?
- How much will it cost the organization?
- What are the tax ramifications?

Enrollment Realities

The first thing that determines how much a plan will cost is how many employees will elect it. Average enrollment in any organization offering these benefits remains at less than 3 percent of the total employee population. The organization can further control enrollment by intentionally limiting the benefits to same-sex partners and their children only.

Common Ground's study undertaken in 1998-1999 revealed that the average enrollment in plans where the total eligible population is between 1,000 and 100,000 is 0.7 to 1 percent in gay-only plans and 2 to 4 percent in plans that include straight people. Only in plans where less than 1,000 or more than 100,000 people are eligible do the "take rates" exceed 1 percent in gay-only plans or 5 percent in straight-included plans. A younger-than-average workforce (i.e., average age is twenty-five or less) may experience higher enrollment numbers, primarily for its heterosexual members.

The question is often asked, "Why do straight couples elect the benefits more often than gay couples do?" The most obvious reason is that there are simply more straight people in the world; at least a 3 to 1 ratio, if not a little more. But there are other reasons:

1. In many straight relationships, married or not, one partner performs the role of housewife or househusband and caretaker (whether there are kids or not). This makes it easier for the employee's partner to qualify for DPBs because the partner's employment status is a big part of the qualification process.

2. In gay relationships, two things are common: both adult partners work and have benefits through their own employers; and because of the tax ramifications of DPBs, even if one partner's plan is "better" than the other's, the imputed value of DPBs would keep a partner from accepting that cost as compared to his or her own free or less expensive (out-of-pocket) plan.

3. As a continuation of point number two above, many organizations will not let a person—spouse, partner, or whoever—join their benefits plan if the person has one slready.

4. Fear of revealing one's orientation is another thing that keeps enrollment—specifically gay enrollment—down. Frankly, even when confidentiality is promised, fear of being outed by the process of electing benefits remains a big problem for many gay people. This is why it is of enormous importance that DPBs not be introduced in a vacuum where no preparations have been made to help members of the organization deal with their issues— pro and con regarding not only the benefits themselves, but also the inexorably connected questions related to sexual orientation and its acknowledgment in work and family programs.

About Adverse Selection

Contrary to warnings and predictions made by insurance companies and other concerned parties since the mid-1980s, extending coverage to partners—specifically gay male partners—has not resulted in increased costs due to "adverse selection," which is a polite term for HIV/AIDS-affected parties.

In no instance where a surcharge was demanded by an insurance carrier or HMO at the start of same-sex partner plans was that surcharge still in force two years later; such surcharges are unheard-of today.

All evidence indicates without exception that not only are partner benefits not more expensive than traditional family benefits, they are actually less expensive. A big part of the reason for this has to do with maternity-related expenses.

When straight couples are included in DPB plans, there will be more people in the plan. But when straight couples decide to add children to their family, they typically get married. This will make that particular couple's participation in the DPB plan moot, but will still incur expenses for the medical benefit plan related to maternity.

As more gay families choose children, and more are every day, they too will begin to constitute an increased expenditure for medical benefits plans; however, this increase in gay families with kids will likely also mirror the legal marriage of gay couples—again, rendering the question of partner benefits moot.

Another fact about DPB plans that not only keeps their cost down but contributes to lower premiums for everyone is that people in partner situations tend to be younger, and younger people tend to be healthier. That means that a healthier population is brought into the group plan, which helps drive premium costs down for everyone. As straight people age, they are more likely to marry and so their effect on the cost of the plans lessens; soon, this will also be true for gay partners in the plan who will opt for marriage or legal partnership, however that shakes out. But for now, these people represent a cost savings for everyone.

In order of cost to health plans, HIV/AIDS ranks fifth behind maternity, heart disease, cancer, and Alzheimer's. There has not been a single case of spiking in a plan's cost due to AIDS anywhere in the United States.

The Cost of DPBs Related to Taxes: For Employers

Employers treat their premium contribution to the domestic partner's coverage as a compensation expense under Code Section 162 (see Appendix A), attributable to the employment of the employee. In other words, they treat it just as they treat premium contributions for legal spouses and dependents. Employers therefore take these premium contributions as tax deductions by classifying them as an "ordinary and necessary business expense."

These actions, to date, are based on private letter rulings (PLRs) issued to organizations by the IRS to employers who have asked for them. A PLR does not, by definition, constitute a precedent, and so a tax attorney should always be consulted, but absent any sweeping rulings by the IRS, organizations with DPBs are operating in this manner.

In those cases where employee benefits premiums are paid from VEBA Trust (Voluntary Employee Benefit Association) accounts, a separate account must be created to pay for nonlegal spouse and dependent benefits. Doing so does not affect the tax status of the payments to the organization.

Taxes: For Employees

The tax picture for employees who elect coverage for their partners is not as favorable (*please note:* this applies to employee discounts as imputable income along with medical/dental benefits). Employees must pay tax on the fair market value of the benefits they elect for their partners. Fair market value will be explained momentarily.

Employer-provided health benefits for partners or nonspouse cohabitants of an employee are excludable from imputed income only if the party qualifies under IRS Code 152 and subsets (see Appendix A). For federal tax purposes, the determination of legal spouse status is based on state marital laws. What constitutes a dependent is determined by state and local law as well as by the definition under the tax codes. If the recipient of the benefit is a legal spouse or dependent, the fair market value of the benefit is considered tax-qualified (no taxes assessed).

Furthermore, in those cases where the employer-provided health care coverage is offered through a flexible benefits plan in which employees contribute to the cost of dependent coverage, the contribution from the employee for his or her partner's or partner's children's coverage must be made with after-tax dollars. This results in the employee being taxed twice on money related to these benefits.

What Is Fair Market Value?

The amount of a benefit that is taxable (imputed) is called its fair market value. Most organizations determine this value by doing a calculation of the full, unsubsidized, individual rate for insurance, less the remainder of subtracting the employee's individual rate from the employee's family rate. In other words, the value is the amount of premium paid by the employer toward the partner's coverage minus whatever the employee contributes toward that coverage.

The following examples demonstrate the current (typical) calculation of fair market value and the after-tax responsibility of the employee to the plan for his or her partner and/or partner's dependents:

	Health	Dental	Vision	Total
Employee	$126.00	$43.09	$7.05	$176.14
Employee + 1	$398.00	$82.30	$15.23	$495.53
Employee + Family	$461.00	$128.23	$15.73	$604.96
Employee + Children	$334.00	$128.23	$15.73	$477.96

Situation 1: You have coverage for yourself and you add a domestic partner.

$496.03 \times 20\% =$ employee contribution of $99.20.

$176.14 \times 20\% =$ employee contribution for self of $35.23.

$99.20 - $35.23 = $63.97 is paid for partner after tax.

Imputed income:

Employer contribution for two people is: $496.03 \times 80\% = $396.82.

Employer contribution for employee only is: $176.14 \times 80\% = $140.91.

$396.82 - $140.91 -$ employee's contribution for self of $35.23 = $220.68 is imputed value per pay period. This number is added to the employee's gross for the period and taxed accordingly. It can be listed as a separate line item if you wish. The result will be the same.

Situation 2: You have coverage for yourself and you add your partner and your partner's child.

$604.96 \times 20\% =$ employee contribution of $120.99.

$120.99 -$ employee's contribution for self of $35.23 = $85.76.

$85.76 ÷ 3 (or whatever number of children added) for the employee, the partner, and the child = $28.58.

$28.58 × 2 (for partner and child) = $57.17. This is the amount paid after tax by the employee with $63.81 paid pretax.

Imputed income:

$604.96 × 80% = employer contribution for family of $483.97.

Minus employer's contribution for the employee = $140.91.

$483.97 − $140.91 = $343.06 is the amount added to the employee's gross for the period and taxed accordingly.

Situation 3: You have coverage for yourself and you add your partner's child only *(for the sake of the exercise, we will assume one child that the partner cannot provide coverage for).*

$477.96 × 20% = employee contribution of $95.59.

$95.59 − employee's contribution for self of $35.23 = $60.36.

$60.36 is paid for child after tax.

Imputed income:

$477.96 × 80% = employer's contribution of $382.37.

Minus employer's contribution for employee self = $140.91.

$382.37 − $140.91 = $241.46 is the amount added to the employee's gross for the period and taxed accordingly.

DETERMINING WHO IS A DOMESTIC PARTNER

The following are common definitions of a domestic partner:

- A relationship resembling a family or household with close cooperation between the parties, who are of the same gender (this naturally is not included where the benefits will be made available to heterosexual couples), each having specified responsibilities.

- A committed, nonplatonic relationship of two parties unrelated to the extent that were legal marriage available to them, they would not be legally prohibited by blood relationship from marrying in the state where they reside.
- Two unrelated individuals who share the necessities of life, live together, and have a documented emotional and financial commitment to each other.

Beyond these definitions, the organization must decide for itself whether an affidavit will be required, whether a time requirement will be stipulated, whether it will also require marriage licenses from heterosexual employees, whether termination affidavits will be required, and under what circumstances another partner could be added to a DPB plan after the termination of a partnership.[7] Last, it must decide whether to include straight couples in the plan too.

Whether straight along with gay people are included in these definitions is entirely up to the organization. The consequences of this decision will be seen, as stated before, in the "take rates" for the benefits, but again, unless the organization employs less than 1,000 or more than 100,000 people, the differences are negligible.

If the organization's nondiscrimination policy makes reference to sexual orientation (we all have one), gender, marital status, compensation, and/or benefits, it may be well advised to be as inclusive as possible. Frankly, there are thousands of organizations whose nondiscrimination statements say all of these things, but they still don't have partner benefits. These thousands are operating in violation of their own policies and ought to take a close look at that.

Who Constitutes a Dependent?

The party (usually a parent by birth, by marriage, or by other legal procedure such as an adoption) who contributes at least 51 percent of a minor's support is the parent who can/will legally claim the minor as a dependent for tax purposes. This will impact the status of some benefits as applicable to a DPB plan if the organization wishes to use the legal definition of dependent as its definition of dependent.

However, the organization is free to define dependent as it wishes for the purpose of DPBs as long as tax requirements are fulfilled and service venders (such as stop-gap insurers, day-care referral agencies, etc.) cooperate.

Miscellaneous (but Important) Details

Fraud

Not a single case of fraud perpetrated by a person or partnership (gay or straight) has been documented in any DPB plan in the United States since 1982. All fraud in benefits plans appears to be committed by people claiming to be legally married who are not. Affidavits of partnership make it very difficult and very unwise to elect DPBs for which the parties do not qualify.

Termination of Benefits

In almost all cases of partnership termination, the employee is required to notify the employer in writing. In some cases (and this is recommended for the protection of the nonemployee partner) an affidavit of termination will be signed by both parties. Common Ground recommends the use of a termination affidavit even in those situations where an affidavit of partnership is not required.

It is not unusual for an employee who terminates a domestic partnership to have to wait three months, six months, or even a year before enrolling a new partner. This is in contrast to heterosexual married people who can, if they wish, divorce and remarry in much shorter time frames. Whether or not to require a "buffer" between the termination of one partnership and the establishment of another for the purposes of benefits is up to the employer.

The termination agreement need not be complex or convoluted. It should simply assert that the partnership has ended (whether the ending is amicable is not the point) and that the partner understands that his or her health/dental insurance and status as beneficiary of other DPB plan provisions will end as of a given date. It is not unusual for a COBRA-like extension of up to ninety days to be offered the partner to give him or her time to secure other insurance.

WINNING PARTNER BENEFITS

The first step toward implementing domestic partner benefits is to win upper management's approval of the concept and then of the actual plan. Getting these people on board is the only way to ensure the proposal's success. Whether it is one highly interested senior manager or an entire task force, management's support will depend on being provided with the answers to two basic questions:

1. How much is this going to cost?
2. Exactly why should we do this?

Whether you or someone you hire broaches this idea to management, arguments and data about those two things should figure prominently. All arguments must be based on fact, not emotion. The concept of fairness is an appropriate subtle theme, but arguments related to profitability, competitive and market advantages, and productivity will get the proposal much further. The presenter must be absolutely up to date on all cost figures, statistics, and relevant equations. Senior managers will not seriously consider any proposal that leaves them with a lot of action items; you must leave them with only decision points.

Consultants

It is at this juncture that many organizations find it more efficient and effective to turn to a consultant. It's efficient because a consultant specializing in domestic partner benefits will have all the pertinent information at hand and can therefore save management a lot of time. It's effective because use of a consultant removes emotion from the equation.

Any time an organization is considering a progressive step such as the implementation of domestic partner benefits, it is making a very significant statement about the organization as a whole. The decision whether to implement benefits will have ramifications for the enterprise both internally and, externally. Internally, the organization is sending a clear message to all its personnel about how it views equitable treatment, and, externally, the organization is making a statement to society as a whole about its values and how it intends to conduct itself.

Whether a consultant is utilized or a task force of concerned personnel and management comes together to influence policy, the first step is to make sure that the company's nondiscrimination policy expressly includes sexual orientation. That is the foundation upon which any rational argument for the implementation of the benefits—in whatever form—must be built.

People will argue that it is easier to win these benefits in the "more liberal" areas of the United States, such as the Northeast and the West Coast. Interestingly, this statement is much less true now than it was even five years ago because what's driving the move toward DPBs is completely involved in profitability, competitive and market advantages, and productivity.

The point is, if people stick to facts and logic and utilize the services of a consultant with these tools, they stand an excellent chance of winning the benefits regardless of their geographic location.

Any single employee can be the impetus to start this ball rolling. Any employee can reach out to others to establish a task force, or can approach the human resources department and ask for help. The amount of personal involvement is a matter of individual preference. It is true that a certain amount of courage is involved, but persistence and reaching out to resources both inside and outside the company are the real keys to success.

What to Include in the Proposal

Relevant management should be presented with facts and figures that address the proposed benefits, including (in the following order):

1. The definition of domestic partner benefits
2. A justification for their implementation at your organization
3. The meaning of a nondiscrimination policy that expressly includes sexual orientation
4. Requirements for qualification as a domestic partner
5. A recommendation of which benefits currently offered to legal spouses and/or dependents would be extended to partners and/or their dependents
6. Examples of the projected cost of the benefits to the company
7. Examples of the projected cost of the benefits to the employees who elect them
8. An explanation and example of the tax ramifications to all parties
9. Explanation of how the implementation of these benefits would affect the enterprise
10. Information about the position of the insurance industry in general, and your insurers in particular, in regard to these benefits

11. A detailed plan to handle registration for and administration of these benefits
12. A detailed plan for the communication of the benefits plan to all employees and (if desired) to the outside world

Implementation Considerations

Communications

Human resources must take care that all communications from it to all employees stress diversity by way of both their content and choice of words. Organizations go to great lengths to use the correct words when referring to gender, race, ethnicity, and religious affiliation. Sexual orientation is no different. The word *spouse,* for example, is intrinsically tied to the concept of legal marriage; therefore, the word *partner* in its place or certainly in addition, is more appropriate.

Education

It is impossible to overemphasize the importance or effectiveness of educational programs focused on sexual orientation issues in the workplace. Once a program is developed, all of management should be encouraged—if not mandated—to attend and should be further encouraged to enable their personnel to attend. If this proves impossible or impractical for your environment, you might consider bringing a number of regional human resources staff up to speed on sexual orientation issues as they regard strict workplace issues and domestic partner benefits so that these people may be fully prepared to deal with issues should they arise. Common Ground always recommends that as a bare minimum requirement, and absent a formal educational initiative, at least one person in each region should be completely aware of the motives and particulars of the organization's decision to implement partner benefits.

Awareness Raising Programs

Some degree of coordination can take place between headquarters and field human resources staff to develop and participate in regularly scheduled (perhaps monthly) brown bag lunch programs to engender dialogue on this subject, under the supervision of a diversity specialist and/or professional facilitator. These programs could feature guest speakers, movies, other programs, books, and so forth.

Chapter 7

Legalized Same-Sex Relationships and Their Effect on Employment

We hold that the State is constitutionally required to extend to same-sex couples the common benefits and protections that flow from marriage under Vermont law. The extension of the Common Benefits Clause (of the Vermont State Constitution) to acknowledge the plaintiffs as Vermonters who seek nothing more, nor less, than legal protection and security for their avowed commitment to an intimate and lasting human relationship is simply, when all is said and done, a recognition of our common humanity. *

Some, the authors included, would say that in passing the final structure for the implementation of their decision to the legislature, i.e., whether to grant full and equal marriage licenses to nonheterosexual couples or create some sort of a parallel universe called "legal domestic partnership," the judges of the Vermont Supreme Court abdicated their responsibility to answer the question completely and finish the matter, at least in Vermont, once and for all. Even one of the justices herself, Denise R. Johnson, believed that the court should have gone further and immediately allowed lesbian and gay couples to marry in civil ceremonies on par with their heterosexual counterparts.

History has taught us much, though we as a race continually seem deaf and blind to its lessons when it suits us. One thing that it has tried

---

*From the decision of the Vermont Supreme Court, December 1999, mandating that the Vermont State Legislature would extend to lesbian and gay couples the same rights, protections, benefits, and obligations available to nongay couples through marriage.

to teach us, especially in the United States of America, is that separate but equal is never equal. We seem destined over the next few years to learn this lesson again when it comes to civil marriage and all its import to individuals in a free society and to the society itself.

This chapter is not, however, about the lessons that will be learned. It's about the issues and challenges that will confront employers of all kinds (primarily in the United States) as these lessons are being learned—likely repeatedly, and likely state by state (or common-wealth).

We will address the following:

- What marriage is
- Civil marriage versus domestic partnership
- Why people legally marry and what their marriages mean
- The effect of legal relationships on workplace performance: Their place in the national psyche
- Same-sex marriage and the workplace—issues and challenges

WHAT MARRIAGE IS

The definition of *marriage,* according to the *American Heritage Dictionary,* is: (1) The condition of being married; wedlock. (2) A wedding ceremony. (3) A close or intimate union.[1]

And if you continue down the road of definition to such words as *wedded, wedlock, wed, husband, wife, ceremony,* and so forth, you will not come across any definition of any word, in or out of the context of matrimony (including the word *matrimony* itself), that requires a male-female or heterosexual relationship between the (two) parties involved. In fact, gay people get married all the time, just not in concert with their sexual orientation and likely not in the best interest of either party.[2]

At the turn of the twenty-first century, the Church or Temple (choose any denomination, it barely matters) would have it that marriage is for a single man and a single woman and always has been. Neither statement is true. Mormonism has in the past and in some schools continues to embrace polygamy, and John Boswell's work related to Christianity, Catholicism, and the religious history of marriage in those doctrines offers significant proof that not only were same-sex marriages or unions sanctioned by the Church, but male/male marriages were the first such sanctified relationships in the history of the Church.[3] Given the way major religions have treated and continue to treat women as a whole, nothing could be less surprising.

What's important about this for the purposes of this discussion is that there is very definitely a difference between legal marriage or a legal relationship and what is considered "marriage" by a given religion. The latter is not part of our discussion from this point forward as it is easy to be legally married in the United States without ever setting foot in a church or a temple.

In finding without exception, until the Vermont court handed down its decision, that gay couples could not marry because their relationships did not fit the "recognized definition" of marriage[4]—one man married to one woman—the courts in the United States turned a blind eye to the fact that this has never been the wholly recognized definition of marriage at all, not even in the United States. Marriage has served to substantiate claims of property ownership, ownership of a person (man owning his wife), inheritance or rights to title, and things of that nature. It has also been tied to claims of substantiating love forever after and the responsibility of the parties to procreate.

This last was used as recently as the announcement of the Vermont decision by President Clinton who said he was all for equal status for gays and lesbians, but that he thinks marriage is for the procreation of children. He thankfully didn't insult our intelligence by mentioning fidelity nor did he, and this is interesting given his genuine interest in genetic research, offer an opinion as to the marital status of heterosexual couples who get help from their local laboratory, which is something that gay couples also do with great frequency to procreate. And he conveniently leaves out all those heterosexual couples that choose not to parent in any way. One does not imagine for a moment that Mr. Clinton would suggest that childless, heterosexual couples are not "really married."

Given even this basic discussion, the reader can appreciate how complex, convoluted, and, admittedly, interesting the whole debate can be, and so we return our focus to the import and impact of legal relationships and the workplace.

CIVIL MARRIAGE
VERSUS DOMESTIC PARTNERSHIP

Legal marriage affects and is affected by approximately 1,043 federal laws, statutes, and the like, and it also impacts 150 to 250 laws in each U.S. state or commonwealth. Marriage laws are at the sole discretion of each state with, as noted previously, no religious requirements. In fact, you can legally marry in the United States even if you have committed capital crimes and even if you are incarcerated for the duration of your marriage. A marriage is a legal marriage even if it has not been consummated.

Some states (Alaska, Colorado, Iowa, Kansas, Montana, Oklahoma, Pennsylvania, Rhode Island, South Carolina, Texas, Utah, New Hampshire [for inheritance purposes only], and the District of Columbia) recognize common-law marriage. Like marriage as a result of a civil ceremony, these are currently also only the purview of heterosexual couples, and as with civil-ceremony marriages, common-law marriages that are valid in one of these twelve states and the District of Columbia are similarly recognized as valid in the thirty-eight states that don't make provisions for common-law marriage. With some caveats, a common-law marriage is marriage in the United States.

Legal status as a domestic partner as opposed to legal marriage status differs in that:

- Partnerships do not bear the same weight of social acceptance as marriage relationships.
- Partnerships bear standards of proof (length of relationship, for example) that are far beyond what is required to get legally married (for instance, a legally married couple doesn't even have to live together to be married).
- Partnerships are granted no recognition beyond the jurisdiction that offers them.
- Partnerships have a separate and unequal, second-class citizen status.
- Partnerships can be voted out of existence by popular referendum (as in Hawaii).

- Partnerships carry no legal precedents upon which to base other decisions of import between two people in a committed relationship unless other significant documentation is procured and produced.
- Even if documentation is procured and produced, the nonlegal status of a partnership is no guarantee that a legal relationship would not be found to supersede the partnership (i.e., parent, sibling, ex-spouse, child).
- Domestic partner status is back-of-the-bus thinking. Such thinking is no less unacceptable to affected parties now than it was in the 1950s.
- Domestic partnership status, implied as separate from and not equal to legal marriage as recognized in all fifty states, would be at the discretion of legislatures and popular votes nationwide. This would put these relationships at a severe disadvantage if the parties wished to relocate, or even simply travel, throughout the country.
- Absent full, equal marriage rights, it is also doubtful that a separate structure of relationship can or will even come close to replicating the more than 1,000 federal rights and responsibilities of legal marriage or the 150 to 250 in each of the fifty states.

These last two represent the bulk of potential problems for employers, especially those who do business in more than one state. Even though more than thirty states and the federal government have enacted laws that vacate their obligation to honor legal same-sex relationships in any of the other fifty states (a.k.a. DOMA or the Defense of Marriage Act), it remains unclear at this writing whether these acts are themselves legal under the full faith and credit clause of our Constitution that speaks to the recognition of licenses in one state that have been issued in another.

Imagine how difficult our lives would be in the United States if our driver's licenses issued in Colorado were invalidated in Kansas as soon as we crossed the state line on our way to Ohio. Our society faces the same kind of conundrum relative to same-sex relationships enjoying full recognition in some jurisdictions but not others. And we faced the same conundrum when dealing with interreligious marriage, interracial marriage, and divorce decrees issued in one state, but not recognized in others.

It is also true that, at last count, approximately 1,500 marriages in the United States at the beginning of the twenty-first century are, in fact, same-sex marriages and are fully legal. What typically transpired in these cases is that a heterosexual man married a heterosexual woman and then underwent transition as a transsexual to become a woman. This change in sex did not affect the validity of the marriage and therefore, they are legal same-sex marriages.

WHY PEOPLE LEGALLY MARRY AND WHAT THEIR MARRIAGES MEAN

The figure of 1,043 federal laws affecting rights and responsibilities tied to marital status is the result of a search by the General Accounting Office in 1997 or 1998 during the time when it appeared that Hawaii might become the first state to recognize marriage between persons of the same sex. The government wanted to know, logically, what in our society actually would be affected by such a change in legal marriage. Many people were interested in this question, it turns out, none more so than the people fighting for the ability to benefit from marital rights and live up to marital responsibilities. For this reason, it likely remains true that the people who know the most about legal marriage in the United States are the people who can't get legally married—at least not to their same-sex partners—unless they wish to deny their sexual orientation.

In our education courses, we often ask the married people in the room if they know what they signed up for when they said "I do" in front of the justice of the peace or when they signed the marriage license prior to their appearance at the altar or under the canopy. We've never yet, in three years, encountered a single married heterosexual who knew about the number and scope of their federal and state obligations under the marriage laws. This is almost as sad as the fact that less than 30 percent of eligible adults bother to vote. It's infuriating to those who can't marry because the blockage to same-sex marriage is perpetrated mostly by people who don't have the faintest idea what they are talking about in the first place. Another one of life's unfunny ironies.

People get married today for the same reasons that they always have: because it's expected of them; because they're in love; because the other party has something they want; because they are about to start a family whether they planned to or not; because they're lonely; etc. Frankly, people enter into domestic partnerships—same-sex based or otherwise—for many of the same reasons. It's a human thing. But absent the ability to get married, people in thoughtful, committed relationships should, perhaps must, and certainly often do, go out of their way to make provisions to protect the relationship legally, financially, and in terms of their fiduciary responsibility to one another.

These provisions include wills, powers of attorney, health care proxies, living wills, bank or other joint financial accounts, trusts, and joint deeds of property ownership. All of them are also duplicated by some married couples, but the majority of what is covered in all of them is implied by the civil marriage contract unless other arrangements are specified by the parties. This again reinforces the point made above that you can, in a legal marriage, release yourself and/or your spouse from any number of legal, financial, fiduciary, or even residence responsibilities and still remain legally married. Partners cannot do any of that.

And, because partners have no other way to obtain these protections, real or implied, people in same-sex committed relationships spend an inordinate amount of money trying to replicate what our heterosexual counterparts get after a forty-dollar blood test, a signature, and saying "I do." Some states don't even mandate the blood test anymore.

Beyond this, there are things that partners cannot, under any circumstances, replicate for the protection of themselves or their partners no matter how much money they spend or who their lawyer is:[5]

- Automatic assumption of spouse's pension (including IRAs, Roth IRAs, 401K plans)
- Automatic inheritance, including associated tax breaks and access to gift tax relief
- Automatic housing lease transfer
- Bereavement leave
- Burial determination
- Certain property rights

- Child custody
- Crime victim recovery benefits
- Domestic violence protection
- Exemption from property tax on partner's death
- Immunity from testifying against partner in legal matters
- Insurance breaks (property, life, disability)
- Joint adoption (except in New Jersey as of January 2000) and foster care
- Joint bankruptcy
- Joint parenting
- Reduced-rate memberships
- Sick leave to care for partner
- Visitation of partner's children
- Visitation of partner in hospital or prison
- Wrongful death (loss of consort) benefits
- Social Security benefits

This is only a partial list, and admittedly leaves out some of the downside to legal marriage, such as the so-called marriage penalty relative to federal income taxes . . . and formal in-laws visiting for the holidays. But if any couple crunches the numbers, they will find that what they gain as per all this list significantly outweighs what it costs in terms of such things as the marriage penalty, both in terms of dollars and in terms of the social status conferred by legal marriage in the United States.

Why do people get married? Usually for love, occasionally for less noble reasons. What does their marriage mean? Typically much more than they ever imagined.

THE EFFECT OF LEGAL RELATIONSHIPS ON WORKPLACE PERFORMANCE: THEIR PLACE IN THE NATIONAL PSYCHE

From 1994 to 1998, the number of Americans living in unmarried-partner households increased at five times the rate of married-couple households.[6] In a recent survey conducted by a Columbia University political scientist, the following was found to be true:[7]

- Women and people of color are consistently more supportive of equal employment rights and antidiscrimination laws than are white male Americans.
- 55 percent of those surveyed reported having a gay friend or acquaintance; this was a 12 percent increase in less than four years.
- 70 percent think gay people should be able to serve their country openly.
- 75 percent support the hiring of gay/lesbian doctors; this up from 53 percent five years earlier.
- Solid majorities support gay inheritance rights and Social Security benefits for gay couples.

In 1998, only 33 percent or less of those surveyed believed that gay people would ever be allowed to enter into legal marriage. In December of 1999, according to a *Wall Street Journal*/NBC News poll, that number is now 66 percent and climbing. Why is this? Because we, as a society, support and believe in the family, and because we, again as a society, are starting to recognize that families come in all forms.

The percentage of people who now favor, or at least would tolerate, legal same-sex marriage continues to rise at about the rate and over the same time period as did the acknowledgement of most Americans that people deserve equitable protections and benefits in the workplace, regardless of sexual orientation. That took a number of years to sink in; same-sex marriage rights are new and will also take a number of years to sink in.

In a report issued by Professor Michael Wald of Stanford University that explored the effects of legal same-sex marriage on "the family" including and perhaps especially on children, he found that, drawing on studies by the American Psychological Association, among others, children raised by gay parents are as well off as children raised by heterosexual parents.[8] The courts in Hawaii came to the same conclusion, even though there it went for naught.

Looking at a DOMA-type bill in California at the time, and trying to assess the act's eventual ability to achieve its goal of "promoting stability and well being for children through marriage," Wald concluded that acts such as DOMA do exactly the opposite. They stigmatize same-sex couples, destroy the emotional well-being of the children from same-sex households, and destabilize the financial security of these families. In short, passage of DOMA-like laws only add to family pressures and stress, and children feel all of it.

Adults feel it too, which is why marriage in general has been proven good both for a society and also for the individuals who enter into such unions. Such relationships contribute to better physical and emotional health, higher self-esteem, greater stability, and the ability to pay more attention to tasks outside of the marriage given a solid foundation from which to operate. Married employees are, for the most part, better and more reliable employees, and organizations should encourage—not be part of any movement to discourage—people to marry based on that criterion alone.

SAME-SEX MARRIAGE AND THE WORKPLACE: ISSUES AND CHALLENGES

Should same-sex marriage be afforded legal status in at least one state, or should a form of domestic partnership be afforded to persons in one state with the possibility of their legal transference to others, employers of all kinds will be faced with the following:

1. Same-sex marriage on a par with current legal marriage (that is, between a man and a woman who are presumed to be heterosexual) will mean that employers in the state that recognizes these marriages will have to abide by state law as regards hard benefits, pensions, Social Security withholding, taxes, nondiscrimination statutes, insurance, family leave, bereavement leave, child care, cafeteria-plan benefits, employee discount or lease programs, COBRA benefits; in short, all of the typical workplace benefits that are afforded employees based on marital status. However, they will also have to abide by the laws of a federal government that will not recognize these marriages as legal. Therefore, there will have to be separate administration of these matters for state and federal purposes.

2. Employees in that state who believe themselves to be legally married in every sense will likely not abide by a system of different treatment for state and federal purposes. A likely rationale will be that marriage rights are states' rights and the federal government has no basis upon which not to recognize them. In fact, the only reason DOMA has not been challenged is for simple lack of a same-sex

marriage to bring to bear on the federal government, marriages of transgender persons notwithstanding. Employers will be in the middle of this issue and may find themselves party to class actions that seek to rectify it.

3. Should one state in which the employer does business legalize same-sex marriages and should one or more other states decide to recognize those marriages as legal, then the employer will have to maintain different standards for employees in any number of states *and* also differentiate workplace benefits matters for the federal government. For example, upon hearing of the decision in Vermont, even though marriage versus partnership was not resolved, parties in Pennsylvania, New Jersey, and Rhode Island immediately saw similarities in their state constitutions to that of Vermont upon which to mount similar legal actions.

4. Some states, with precedent or not, will see the wisdom both philosophically and financially in recognizing same-sex marriages performed in other states even if they don't immediately allow such marriages to take place within them. Again, such actions will force employers to make different provisions for people in different places—not a very practical way to do business, with potentially damaging effects of litigation time and funds.

5. Beyond benefits, employers would have problems relocating an employee if an employee were faced with changing his or her marital status upon accepting a relocation. The discrimination potential here is considerable.

6. Should legal domestic partnership become law in a state, Vermont for example, the employer faces the same conundrum as in all of the preceding items if only because matters related to separate but unequal status will engender additional suits and efforts to gain similar or better status by other people in other states.

The workplace figures to be a place, perhaps *the* place, where the issue of same-sex legal relationships gets the most attention. First, we all spend a great deal of time at work, which ensures interaction and dialogue on the subject. Because so much about marriage is misunderstood, some of this dialogue will be filled with rancor, and that will not be good for business, whatever the business is.

Second, marriage is (like so many things) very much about money. Of the 1,043 federal laws and 150 to 250 state laws regarding marriage in the United States, well over two-thirds concern themselves with finance. To pretend that this is not of paramount importance to people—especially working people—is irresponsible and ridiculous.

It is in the best interest of everyone that legal same-sex marriage be institutionalized throughout the United States as soon as possible. Everything from history to public opinion to the continued welfare and betterment of our society makes such legalization inevitable someday. If that day were sooner rather than later, a great deal of time, money, and effort would not go misspent.

Chapter 8

The FAQs of the Matter

In this chapter we provide brief answers to the questions most frequently asked about gays insofar as the workplace is concerned. A couple of these step outside that strict boundary, but the answers to them affect what happens at many workplaces and so we have retained them. We have also created a separate section for questions related to domestic partner benefits. Much more comprehensive information about everything included here is part of the preceding chapters.

FAQs ABOUT GAYS AND THE WORKPLACE

Do gays want "special rights"?

No. They want the same rights that others enjoy. The rights of Americans, civil and otherwise, are (as of this writing) specifically protected on the basis of sexual orientation in only eleven states: California, Connecticut, Hawaii, Massachusetts, Minnesota, Nevada, New Hampshire, New Jersey, Rhode Island, Vermont, and Wisconsin. The protections extended to people on the basis of sexual orientation in these eleven states cover employment, housing, public accommodations, and credit. All state laws relative to sexual orientation specifically exempt insurance and benefits, but two of the eleven, California and Vermont, also offer benefits to state workers and their partners regardless of sexual orientation, gender, and/or marital status.

Some eighteen to twenty states and roughly 300 other jurisdictions within states have executive orders or ordinances (that carry much less weight than law) which provide some level of protection, usually limited to employment, to citizens on the basis of their orientation.

Some people argue that gays want "special rights" because their rights are already protected by the U.S. Constitution. They are not. The equal protection clause of the U.S. Constitution is intended to protect all citizens, but some groups fall into what are known as "suspect classes." The suspect classes recognized today are differentiated by race, national ancestry, and ethnic origin. It is this lack of specified protection that makes it perfectly legal in the majority of the United States for people, typically nonheterosexual people, to be refused employment, refused public accommodation, denied housing, or have their children taken away simply on the basis of their real or perceived orientation. It is also this lack of protection that makes it legal for nonheterosexuals to be hounded from military service and for legislatures to perceive a legal basis on which to pass obnoxious laws such as the Defense of Marriage Act. DOMA remains to be challenged until there is a precedent (i.e., a same-sex marriage legally performed in a state or commonwealth) upon which to issue such a challenge.

No federal job protection is extended to gay and lesbian citizens in the United States. As of this writing, a federal act to implement such protection, the Employment Non-Discrimination Act, remains in Congressional committee.

Last, this lack of federal protection also leads to the almost continuous attempt by people professing to act in the name of religion to withhold civil marriage or legal relationship, employment, accommodation, and other rights from Americans on the basis of their orientation. They never let the fact that they speak for only a particular interpretation of religion or morality stand in their way, and their small, mean-spirited, and hateful actions make legal protection as provided to all other Americans particularly necessary for nonheterosexual citizens.

What if I work in human resources or diversity management, or in organizational development or educational services at an organization, and I don't think we should specify programs or policies to include sexual orientation?

It is our opinion that most leaders of most organizations disapprove of discrimination against their nonheterosexual employees or employees with a nonmajority gender identification. We also believe that most professionals in the area of human resources/training and development do not support discrimination against their co-workers on this or any other basis, but that many are hesitant to take a leadership position in proactively ensuring that such discrimination does not occur. But frankly, and usually to our dismay, we have also met human resources/diversity and training personnel who don't understand a need to include sexual orientation or gender identification in their initiatives and who further don't think it should be included.

It is the role of human resources/diversity or organization development professionals to be able to represent the requirements of all of their co-workers, and to do so proactively before trouble occurs. Those who do not see the need to include sexual orientation or gender identification in these efforts have an obligation to learn more about the subject so as to be able to do their jobs. If they feel that their personal value or belief systems preclude them from finding ways to balance their beliefs with their professional responsibilities regardless of how much information they are given, and if they are unable to live up to all facets of the organization's nondiscrimination policy, then they need to find another line of work.

Since gays are such a minority, why should we include them in our diversity plans?

It does not matter whether there are ten gay people in the country or 10 million. It is wrong to discriminate against anyone on the basis of an inherent characteristic that has no bearing on performance.

However, if you believe that numbers matter, you should recognize that nonheterosexuals are thought to constitute the largest workplace minority.[1] Chances are your organization has a good-sized gay constituency in which you have made, and continue to make, a significant investment.

What are the most common objections to including sexual orientation in workplace policies, and how do I deal with them?

The most common objection stems from a misconception of gays' legal rights. As noted in previous chapters, an overwhelming percentage of Americans do not know that workplace discrimination against gay people is, to a great extent, legal. Therefore, they believe that gays are trying to get special rights or provisions on the basis of a lifestyle choice.

Second, people who do not believe that homosexuality is an inherent characteristic similar to handedness or eye color believe that gays make a conscious choice to be different and therefore are not entitled to minority status.

Third, people hold a belief that lesbians and gays are an economically and educationally elite minority who don't need civil protection or rights because they already have special advantages not available to heterosexuals.

Fourth, people object to anything that might be construed as validation or acceptance of homosexuality because of their religious beliefs. On the other hand, many object to including homosexuals in any workplace diversity programs because there are not enough of them to warrant attention. These are contradictory objections since people with religious or moral concerns spend an inordinate amount of time, money, and energy trying to defeat gay rights initiatives.

Last, people object to inclusion of sexual orientation because of their fear of a human characteristic they don't understand and because of the anger they feel at the discomfort it causes them. The only effective way to combat this objection, and indeed all of them, is to avail yourself of education and information about this issue so that you can respond with facts to objections usually founded on myths and misinformation. Furthermore, you can encourage your company to make sure these facts are available through workplace education, and you can encourage people within your sphere of influence to take advantage of programs that are offered.

If I support inclusion of sexual orientation in my workplace diversity programs, will my company suffer in the marketplace?

There is no evidence to suggest that being supportive of sexual orientation in workplace programs, whether in the form of nondiscrimination policies, educational initiatives, or benefits policies, results in loss of market share or revenues for the organization. In fact, overwhelming evidence suggests that the opposite is true. This is covered in some detail in Chapters 1 and 2 of this book.

Must we include sexual orientation in our nondiscrimination policy?

Yes. Because most lesbian, gay, and transgender people live and work in places without such protection, unless the employer provides some level of nondiscrimination protection, gay people can be (and are) routinely separated from their jobs. It's also important that your nondiscrimination policy or code of conduct specify sexual orientation and not lifestyle or preference.

Should our diversity education include sexual orientation?

Yes. Sexual orientation is perceived as a difficult topic to include in diversity education because it raises a number of intensely personal issues and can cause an extreme degree of discomfort. However, the anticipated difficulty is exaggerated, and it pales in comparison to the importance and benefits of doing so. Education is the answer to homophobia, because homophobia results in lessened productivity and profitability of the enterprise, as well as lessened productivity and job satisfaction of everyone employed there. See Chapter 5 for a comprehensive look at workplace education specific to sexual orientation.

If we allow someone who is HIV positive or AIDS affected to work here, will we endanger other workers?

No. HIV is not transmittable through the kind of casual contact that (most) people have at the office or other place of work. Transmission of the HIV virus that can lead to AIDS-defined conditions requires the exchange of blood or other bodily fluids. The virus requires specific conditions to survive, conditions not commonly found in most public surroundings. This means that sharing a keyboard, a telephone, or a bathroom with an HIV-positive person does not put you at risk. A great deal of HIV information relevant to the workplace is provided in Chapter 5.

Please note: The next three questions are also asked and answered in Chapter 5 on sexual orientation in the workplace.

How does the organization ensure that the education effort won't do more harm than good?

We don't believe that education in and of itself ever poses a danger to anyone. But delivered by the wrong people for the wrong reasons and without adequate preparation, education can be devastating to an organization.

One diversity director we know who requested anonymity on this point learned this lesson the very hard way. A particular employee in her company who happened to be gay was also disliked by a number of his colleagues. Being gay was acknowledged as one of the reasons he was disliked, but it was not the only reason. Being gay was, however, the aspect of this individual targeted by those who did not like him. Their gay-bashing and harassment were blatantly discriminatory and obnoxious both to the employee and to management.

Acting in good faith, appropriate company representatives first spoke to each of the harassing employees individually and told them that their continued abuse of the individual for any reason would not be tolerated. Then management attempted to clear the air by sitting all the parties down and allowing them to express themselves. This turned out to be a very big mistake. The director said, "In trying to educate these employees in this situation, we actually made things worse because we allowed peple to express themselves and a lot of what they had to say could only be described as vehemently interpersonally homophobic. We were not prepared to address their homophobia in any constructive way at that time, and the employee who was being harassed suffered further by finding out how pointed and hateful the attitudes of his co-workers were about him."

Does the facilitator of sexual orientation education have to be gay?

When we first wrote this book we said that, "the short answer is no, the longer answer is it wouldn't hurt, and the best answer is yes." We now adjust this answer to be simply, "no."

The reason for this change of heart if you wish to call it that is that education on the topic of sexual orientation is about just that: sexual orientation, and everyone has one. The most important characteristic of a facilitator is not that he be nonheterosexual; the most important characteristic is that he be completely knowledgeable and prepared about the subject, over and above what he will actually teach. People ask some interesting questions and raise some interesting points for discussion. A well-rounded understanding of the topic is what's called for, not status as "a minority."

We have witnessed some of the best facilitation of programs we've helped develop by heterosexual facilitators. The reason these people were so effective was that they worked hard to find areas of relativity between experiences in their lives and what they were trying to get people to relate to in so far as orientation was concerned. Since the majority of their participants were also heterosexual, the bridges these people build by example were strong and powerfully affecting.

We will say, however, that it is also enormously helpful if one or both (in team teaching situations which we do advocate for in train the educator models) facilitators happen not to be nonheterosexual, to have a member of the workforce in that workplace step up and talk about what it's like to be gay or bi or transgender there. Again, this is an area where the employee alliance can make a significant contribution by having as an arm an internal "speaker's bureau." If no such resource is in place at the organization, there are Speaker's Bureaus and other organizations in (typically) metropolitan areas who can lend some support in a given location that hasn't got its own.

Should sexual orientation education be mandatory?

As we reported in the first edition, Rynes and Rosen in their study of workplace diversity education concluded that it should be mandatory for all. We respectfully disagreed then and we still do. Our opinion is that these programs should be mandatory for senior management (however that term is defined by the organization) because these are people with an obligation to make sure that they focus on behavior, not beliefs, in the workplace, but that they should not be mandatory— although freely recommended and attendance encouraged and certainly not blocked—for everyone else.

These arguments go back to the data that indicates a strong desire for these kinds of programs at work in the first place. If you build them, and build them right, people will come . . . of their own accord.

What does it mean to be transsexual?

The correct term is "transgender," not transsexual, because transsexual people are a subset of transgender people.[2]

Transgender is an all-encompassing term for people who are cross-dressers, intersexed people, transsexual, drag queens, transvestites, or transgenderists.

Transsexuals are people whose gender identity does not match their biological sex. Male to female transsexuals are those who begin life with a typical male biology and who identify as girls and then as women. Those individuals who decide to pursue various strategies for bringing their biological sex into agreement with their gender identity are said to be transitioning or transistional transsexuals. Transgenderists are like transsexuals, but choose not to have genital surgery.

Cross-dressers are people whose gender expression is sometimes at odds with their biological sex. Most cross-dressers are males who identify primarily as men, and most are attracted to women. They dress as women on occasion and usually hope to "pass" as women. There are also female cross-dressers.

Transvestite is a psychiatric term for crossdressers, used especially for male cross-dresssers who put on women's clothing for sexual excitement. Most cross-dressers prefer not to be referred to as transvestites (assuming that they are not transvestites, of course.)

Intersexed people, also called intersexuals, are those whose biological sex is not typically male or female. Their gender identity, gender expression, and sexual orientation may be anywhere on those three scales.

Drag queens are usually gay men who dress in women's clothing.

Why should a form of sexual behavior be acknowledged at work?

Sexual orientation and gender identification respectively have nothing to do with sexual behavior—they are intrinsic characteristics of an individual. Any individual who engages in sexual behavior at work, regardless of sexual orientation or gender identification, should be disciplined.

What are, or should be, the goals of a gay/straight employee-management alliance?

- Ensure that the organization's nondiscrimination policy includes the words *sexual orientation*
- Encourage the organization to publicly support ENDA and/or hate crimes legislation
- Help the organization to identify ways to support employees' efforts in the community relative to gay/lesbian/transgender health issues or civil rights that are both economically feasible and engender positive public relations

- Contribute to efforts to develop and implement meaningful education programs on the topic of sexual orientation in the workplace
- Help the organization investigate and implement partner benefits
- Serve on task forces to investigate and propose ways for the organization to engender patronage from the nonheterosexual community (if applicable)
- Work with the company to ensure productive working relationships—perhaps the attainment of common goals or common understanding—with other employee alliances
- Ensure, absolutely, that all employees—regardless of location or job function—are fully informed about the mission of the alliance and have unfettered opportunity to participate as they wish.

FAQS ABOUT DOMESTIC PARTNER BENEFITS

Why is the organization offering domestic partner benefits?

The organization offering these benefits recognizes that it employs people from various backgrounds. All of its employment and nondiscrimination policies specifically state that we do not discriminate in any matter of employment, including benefits, on the basis of (among other things) sexual orientation, gender, or marital status.

Therefore, in an effort to live up to the letter of our policies, in an effort to be as fair and equitable as possible while remaining fiscally solvent and responsible, and in an effort to respond to the requests of many employees who have a legitimate need for these benefits, we are implementing them.

Why are some benefits excluded?

Some benefits are typically excluded from DPB plans for the following reasons:

- Dependent Care Reimbursement Plan: Deductions for dependent care are designed to be made pretax in order to both help the employee put money aside for dependent care and to do so while reducing their income tax burden. However, due to federal tax code, benefits for persons who are not the legal spouse or legal dependent of an employee cannot be provided for pretax. Therefore, there is no benefit for an employee with a nonlegal spouse or nonlegal dependent to provide for those persons in this matter. A private investment plan would be more advantageous.

- Long- and Short-Term Disability: All employees, regardless of family type or marital status, already have equal access to the benefits of this insurance. Legal spouses or legal dependents typically have no additional rights or access under these plans.
- Life Insurance: As with disability, all employees already have equal access to the benefits of this insurance. Any employee, any person for that matter, can name as beneficiary of an insurance policy a person who can demonstrate an "insurable interest." Due to the tax status of life insurance premiums, the employee would have to make the full premium payment on an after-tax basis to purchase term life insurance for partners as for spouses. Some organizations make these plans available; some believe that partners are better off purchasing this term life insurance separately.

What benefits are typically included?

All medical and dental offerings are included (where not prohibited by state laws or insurance regulations). COBRA-like benefits are included, as are FMLA-like benefits. The reason for calling them "COBRA-like" or "FMLA-like" is that, while the federal acts which initiated these coverages do not specifically include nonlegal spouses or dependents, they do not specifically exclude them either. Therefore, private sector and all other nonfederal employers are able to make the provisions of these plans available in DPB plans.

Also offered are pension payouts similar to those provided for spouses (i.e., vested portion to be paid); employee stock ownership similar to that provided for spouses (again, vested shares to revert), adoption assistance, educational assistance, bereavement leaves, and relocation assistance.

What are the tax ramifications of domestic partner benefits?

The election of benefits that have an "imputed fair market value" has serious tax ramifications. Insofar as medical and dental plans are concerned, documents are usually prepared to show each employee what his or her additional income tax will be as a result of electing these benefits. The only way that this additional tax on income can or will be avoided is if the tax code in the United States changes. Having said all this, a decision to elect partner medical benefits should not be made lightly, but they are usually offered for the benefit of those whose families need them.

Why are we offering these benefits to both same- and opposite-sex partners? (where applicable)

Same-sex partners have no other access to these kinds of benefits if they do not have benefits in their place of employment, or if they are not employed at all. Opposite-sex partners could certainly get married to secure these benefits without question, but as this organization's nondiscrimination policy stipulates not only sexual orientation but also gender and marital status, we wish to be as inclusive as possible.

The matter was studied more in terms of the cost to the benefits plan. Usually it is determined that a budget is not put at risk by including all partners in this plan. However, if and when same-sex couples have access to legal marriage that is honored by all states and the federal government (an event likely to take at least five more years), we will discontinue partner benefits because all people would have, through marriage, equal access. It's also possible that eligibility for benefits will look a lot different by 2010 than it does in 2000.

Do I put my employment at risk if I elect these benefits?

No, absolutely not. As with all personnel files, these matters are considered confidential. Organizations that offer these benefits will not usually tolerate discrimination of any kind on any basis.

What are the qualifications for being a domestic partner for purposes of workplace benefits?

In most instances, the employee and partner have to sign an affidavit attesting to aspects of their relationship. They may be required to provide documentation such as bank receipts, mortgage or rent receipts, various insurance policies, or wills to support their claim of a qualifying relationship. Many organizations don't ask for this documentation unless it is requested by the insurer, which is typically the only time it must actually be produced. However, all employees must realize that if the affidavit is signed fraudulently, they put their employment in jeopardy and they would be responsible for all monies expended for the purpose of the "partner's" benefits or those of that person's children.

The length of time over which the relationship will have to be documented is usually three to six months. If the relationship terminates, as with all changes in family status, the employee will be required to notify human resources. To protect the employee's partner, a notice of termination will also have to be filed.

Should one relationship terminate, the employee will usually be subject to another waiting period to assign another partner.

If we offer benefits to partners, will there be less for traditional families?

No. Gay families, including the partnerships and unions entered into by two adults who happen to be gay, the children they bring to the relationship or produce, their values, interdependence, and commitment are exactly the same as those of heterosexual married couples. The fact that the law does not make provisions for gay families is not relevant—at least not to those families. We will all do well to remember that once upon a time, not long ago, interracial marriage was not legal either, and for many of the same reasons being used as obstacles to gay people.

The dynamics of the family are already grossly different from those that were predominant when our existing laws were written. The kinds of nontraditional groups that businesses must account for in their benefit plans include but are not limited to gay families, single-parent families, foster families, physically or mentally challenged people who live together in supportive families, and extended families, to name a few.

In extending benefits to different classifications of family, no one is penalized. In fact, everyone benefits because everyone contributes on a more equal basis to everyone else's care.

Aren't these benefits expensive?

Most employers report no increase in cost to their benefits plans due to the implementation of DPBs, and many, in our experience, don't even track it. The SHRM (Society of Human Resources Management) surveys of their members on this question overwhelmingly find no cost increases attributed to them.

Do most health providers cover DPBs?

These days, the answer is yes. Some HMO/PPO organizations choose not to write these benefits, and some standard insurers also choose not to. There is only one state/commonwealth jurisdiction (Virginia) as of January 2000 that prohibits licensing DPB plans; but when the first edition was published there were six, so progress has been steady.

Even in those jurisdictions where licensing is an issue, the organization can typically license the program elsewhere. In some cases, not all providers the organization uses will be available to all employees in all places, but some form of coverage will be available. Many organizations have, in the last six years, left one provider in favor of another to be able to offer DPBs to their employees, which has contributed to a greater variety of plans being licensed.

Appendix A

Domestic Partner Benefits

TAX CODES

(Author note: The following is provided for informational purposes only. Please be sure to consult a certified tax adviser before making any decisions regarding the taxation of domestic partner benefits.)

IRS Code 162

The employer's cost of domestic partner coverage is a compensation expense under IRS Code Section 162, attributable to the employment of the "employee partner." *Therefore, the expense is tax deductible by the employer. (Author note: Most employers classify their contributions to the partner's and/or the partner's dependent's benefits as a "reasonable and ordinary business expense.")*

IRS Code 152: Section 152(a) General Definition

For purposes of this subtitle, the term "dependent" means any of the following individuals over half of whose support, for the calendar year in which the taxable year of the taxpayer begins, was received from the taxpayer, or is treated under subsection "c" or "e" as received from the taxpayer.

1. a son or daughter of the taxpayer, or a descendant of either.
2. a stepson or stepdaughter of the taxpayer.
3. a brother, sister, stepbrother, or stepsister of the taxpayer.
4. the father or mother of the taxpayer, or an ancestor of either.
5. a stepfather or stepmother of the taxpayer.
6. a son or daughter of a brother or sister of the taxpayer.
7. a brother or sister of the father or mother of the taxpayer.
8. a son-in-law, daughter-in-law, father-in-law, mother-in-law, brother-in-law, or sister-in-law of the taxpayer.

9. an individual (other than the individual who at any time during the taxable year was the spouse, determined without regard to section 7703 [former Code Sec. 143] of the taxpayer) who, for the taxable year of the taxpayer, has as his principal place or abode the home of the taxpayer and is a member of the taxpayer's household.

Section 152(b): Rules Relating to General Definition

For the purposes of this Section, an individual is not a member of the taxpayer's household if at any time during the taxable year the relationship between such individual and the taxpayer is in violation of local law. *(Author note: Orientation does not equal behavior, and certain sexual acts between consenting adults—heterosexual or homosexual—constitute sodomy too. Sodomy statutes have never been used to block DP plans.)*

CAVEATS FOR FURTHER CONSIDERATION

In addition to the IRS Codes, a U.S. Treasury regulation that has been called out in some instances as a way to declare a partner as a dependent. It is known loosely as the "51 percent rule." The Treasury regulations say:

> For purposes of determining whether or not an individual received, for a given calendar year, over half of his support from the taxpayer, there shall be taken in to account the amount of support received from the taxpayer as compared to the entire amount of support which the individual received from all sources, including support which the individual himself supplied. The term "support" includes food, shelter, clothing, medical and dental care, education, and the like. Generally, the amount of an item of support will be the amount of expense incurred by the one furnishing such item. If the item of support furnished an individual is in the form of property or lodging, it will be necessary to measure the amount of such item of support in terms of its fair market value.

This has been taken to mean that your partner can be considered a dependent if you provide more than 50 percent of his or her support, *and* he or she is a member of your household for the entire taxable year, *and* he or she did not make more than $2,350.00 in taxable income for the tax year. This is an extremely difficult set of criteria to meet, and is practically nonexistent for the purposes of avoiding imputed status of workplace domestic partner benefits.

Appendix B

Sample Affidavit for Domestic Partners

We, (employee's name) and (partner's name), certify that we are Domestic Partners as described in the benefits enrollment material of (organization name), and that we are therefore eligible for benefits.

(Author note: If you have a Certificate of Domestic Partnership from a city or municipality authorized to grant same, no other proof shall be necessary. If not, the employer and/or its agents or insurers reserve the right to request proof(s) of the nature described in our domestic partner policy as relates to the definition of a domestic partner.

These proofs typically consist of mortgage/rent receipts for at least the term of relationship required, joint bank account statements, designation of beneficiary on wills, insurance policies, investment holdings, etc.)

1. We have an exclusive committed relationship and we have been in such a relationship for at least six months. *(Author note: This could be one month or twelve months. There is no fixed time frame, nor is a time frame always stipulated.)*
   1a. We are of the same sex *(this is included only if that is a stipulation).*
2. We are responsible for each other's common welfare and financial obligations. We are liable to third parties for any obligations incurred by each other and will continue to be so liable during the period that the nonemployee partner is covered by the benefits program.
3. We share the same principal place of residence and intend to do so indefinitely.
4. We are at least eighteen years old and are both mentally competent to consent and enter into a contract.
5. Neither of us is legally married to anyone else, or has had another domestic partner within the last one (six, eight?) month(s).

6. We are not related by blood to a degree of closeness that would prohibit legal marriage in the state in which we legally reside if that were available to us.

7. We agree to notify the employer if our partnership status changes to such a degree that the nonemployee partner would no longer be entitled to benefits under the plan definition. We agree to notify the company in writing within one month (31 days) of such a change.

8. If such termination of relationship occurs, the employee partner agrees that he or she will not file a subsequent Affidavit of Domestic Partnership for a period of (?) months from the date of notification in writing of the existing partnership's termination unless the affidavit is filed for the same nonemployee partner.

9. We understand that (the employer) is not liable or forced to extend COBRA to the nonemployee partner, but does so by its own choice.

10. We understand and agree that the employee partner can and will make health plan elections on behalf of the nonemployee partner.

11. We understand that under applicable state and federal tax laws, employer contributions for the nonemployee partner's health benefits can result in additional imputed income to the employee and that such tax may not be paid with pretax dollars.

12. We understand that any fraudulent claims of partnership, or any failure to comply with the requirements for plan qualification can result in loss of employment and/or civil action against us to recover losses, fees, premiums, and so on.

13. We understand that some courts recognize nonmarriage relationships, not limited to opposite-sex common-law relationships or opposite-sex domestic partnerships, as the equivalent of legal marriage in terms of establishing and dividing community property.

14. We understand that this document is filed confidentially but may be subject to subpoena.

We have read and we understand the terms and conditions under which this coverage is offered and accepted. We declare that all statements assigned to by us are true and that any or all documents submitted to support these statements, if requested, are also true and verifiable.

Signatures and dates *(Notarization is an option)*

Appendix C

Sample Announcement Form

The following is offered strictly as a sample.

_____ is open enrollment month for our health insurance and other benefits plans.

We are pleased to be able to offer domestic partner benefits to those employees whose relationship with their partner of the same *sex (or opposite sex if applicable)* qualify, and whose partner and family would benefit. These benefits are also available to the legal dependents of the employee's partner.

The benefits that are being extended to domestic partners and their dependents are: (insert list here).

Dependent care/health care spending accounts benefits are not included in the plan because of the tax ramifications of the payroll deductions. Pension and long- and short-term disability benefits are not included per se because all employees, regardless of their marital or partner status, already have equal access to these benefits as constructed in our workplace.

Author note: Life insurance purchase options for partners is under study (due to the tax status of life insurance premiums) and the employee discount program (which would necessitate an update of our tracking system) is also under consideration. Employees will be notified if/when these benefits will become part of our plan. In the meantime, more information about their reasons for exclusion will be made available upon request. (This clause included where applicable.)

The election of domestic partner benefits has serious ramifications and stringent requirements for qualification. All of these are explained in the pages that follow. However, if you have any question about the domestic partner benefits plan, or any of our other employee benefits programs, we hope you will feel free to call (fill in a resource) or to attend one of the benefits open houses at this facility.

Appendix D

Sample Termination Agreement

The employee (name) and his or her Domestic Partner (name) hereby mutually attest to the dissolution of their partnership, said partnership having made the nonemployee partner eligible for Domestic Partner Benefits from (organization name).

The nonemployee partner hereby relinquishes his or her eligibility for Domestic Partner Benefits effective (date).

The nonemployee partner hereby requests/does not request COBRA-like benefits to commence on (date) for the specified allowable time period.

The nonemployee partner can be reached at:

(complete address, e-mail address, phone, and fax numbers as applicable)

for the purposes of setting up the COBRA account and/or for a copy of this organization-executed Termination Agreement of Domestic Partner Benefits.

Signed and dated: (employee)

Signed and dated: (nonemployee partner)

Notarized:

Signed and dated: (organizational representative)

Appendix E

General Employment/ENDA

THE EMPLOYMENT NON-DISCRIMINATION ACT (PROPOSED AS OF 1/1/2000)

ENDA would:

extend federal employment discrimination protections currently provided based on race, religion, sex, national origin, age, and disability to sexual orientation.

block public and private employers, employment agencies, and labor unions from using an individual's sexual orientation as the basis for employment decisions, such as hiring, firing, promotion, or compensation.

allow for the same procedures, and similar, but somewhat more limited, remedies as are permitted under Title VII and the Americans with Disabilities Act (ADA).

apply to Congress, with the same procedures as provided by the Congressional Accountability Act of 1995, and presidential employees, with the same procedures as provided under the Presidential and Executive Office Accountability Act of 1996.

ENDA would not:

cover small businesses with fewer than fifteen employees.

cover religious organizations, including educational institutions substantially controlled or supported by religious organizations. The bill only covers employees whose duties pertain solely to a religious organization's activities that generate profits deemed taxable by the Internal Revenue Service.

Source: <www.hrc.org>.

apply to the uniformed members of the armed forces and thus does not affect current law on lesbians and gay men in the military.

allow for quotas or preferential treatment based on the sexual orientation of the individual.

allow a disparate impact claim such as is available under Title VII of the Civil Rights Act of 1964.

allow the imposition of affirmative action for a violation of this Act.

allow the Equal Employment Opportunity Commission (EEOC) to collect statistics on sexual orientation or compel employers to collect such statistics.

apply retroactively.

Appendix F

The Hate Crimes Bill
(Proposed As of 1/1/2000)

A BILL

To enhance Federal enforcement of hate crimes, and for other purposes.

Be it enacted by the Senate and House of Representatives of the United States of America in Congress assembled,

SECTION 1. SHORT TITLE

This Act may be cited as the "Hate Crimes Prevention Act of 1999."

SEC. 2. FINDINGS

Congress finds that—

(1) the incidence of violence motivated by the actual or perceived race, color, national origin, religion, sexual orientation, gender, or disability of the victim poses a serious national problem;

(2) such violence disrupts the tranquility and safety of communities and is deeply divisive;

(3) existing Federal law is inadequate to address this problem;

(4) such violence affects interstate commerce in many ways, including—

  (A) by impeding the movement of members of targeted groups and forcing such members to move across State lines to escape the incidence or risk of such violence; and

  (B) by preventing members of targeted groups from purchasing goods and services, obtaining or sustaining employment, or participating in other commercial activity;

(5) perpetrators cross State lines to commit such violence;

(6) instrumentalities of interstate commerce are used to facilitate the commission of such violence;

(7) such violence is committed using articles that have traveled in interstate commerce;

(8) violence motivated by bias that is a relic of slavery can constitute badges and incidents of slavery;

(9) although many State and local authorities are now and will continue to be responsible for prosecuting the overwhelming majority of violent crimes in the United States, including violent crimes motivated by bias, Federal jurisdiction over certain violent crimes motivated by bias is necessary to supplement State and local jurisdiction and ensure that justice is achieved in each case;

(10) Federal jurisdiction over certain violent crimes motivated by bias enables Federal, State, and local authorities to work together as partners in the investigation and prosecution of such crimes; and

(11) the problem of hate crime is sufficiently serious, widespread, and interstate in nature as to warrant Federal assistance to States and local jurisdictions.

SEC. 3. DEFINITION OF HATE CRIME

In this Act, the term "hate crime" has the same meaning as in section 280003(a) of the Violent Crime Control and Law Enforcement Act of 1994 (28 U.S.C. 994 note).

SEC. 4. PROHIBITION OF CERTAIN ACTS OF VIOLENCE

Section 245 of title 18, United States Code, is amended—

(1) by redesignating subsections (c) and (d) as subsections (d) and (e), respectively; and

(2) by inserting after subsection (b) the following:

"(c)(1) Whoever, whether or not acting under color of law, willfully causes bodily injury to any person or, through the use of fire, a firearm, or an explosive device, attempts to cause bodily injury to any person, because of the actual or perceived race, color, religion, or national origin of any person—

"(A) shall be imprisoned not more than 10 years, or fined in accordance with this title, or both; and

"(B) shall be imprisoned for any term of years or for life, or fined in accordance with this title, or both if—

"(i) death results from the acts committed in violation of this paragraph; or "(ii) the acts committed in violation of this paragraph include kidnapping or an attempt to kidnap, aggravated sexual abuse or an attempt to commit aggravated sexual abuse, or an attempt to kill.

"(2)(A) Whoever, whether or not acting under color of law, in any circumstance described in subparagraph (B), willfully causes bodily injury to any person or, through the use of fire, a firearm, or an explosive device, attempts to cause bodily injury to any person, because of the actual or perceived religion, gender, sexual orientation, or disability of any person—

"(i) shall be imprisoned not more than 10 years, or fined in accordance with this title, or both; and

"(ii) shall be imprisoned for any term of years or for life, or fined in accordance with this title, or both, if—

"(I) death results from the acts committed in violation of this paragraph; or

"(II) the acts committed in violation of this paragraph include kidnapping or an attempt to kidnap, aggravated sexual abuse or an attempt to commit aggravated sexual abuse, or an attempt to kill.

"(B) For purposes of subparagraph (A), the circumstances described in this subparagraph are that—

"(i) in connection with the offense, the defendant or the victim travels in interstate or foreign commerce, uses a facility or instrumentality of interstate or foreign commerce, or engages in any activity affecting interstate or foreign commerce; or

"(ii) the offense is in or affects interstate or foreign commerce."

SEC. 5. DUTIES OF FEDERAL SENTENCING COMMISSION

(a) AMENDMENT OF FEDERAL SENTENCING GUIDELINES— Pursuant to its authority under section 994 of title 28, United States Code, the United States Sentencing Commission shall study the issue of adult recruitment of juveniles to commit hate crimes and shall, if appropriate, amend the Federal sentencing guidelines to provide sentencing enhancements (in addition to the sentencing enhancement provided for the use of a minor during the commission of an offense) for adult defendants who recruit juveniles to assist in the commission of hate crimes.

(b) CONSISTENCY WITH OTHER GUIDELINES—In carrying out this section, the United States Sentencing Commission shall—

(1) ensure that there is reasonable consistency with other Federal sentencing guidelines;

(2) avoid duplicative punishments for substantially the same offense.

SEC. 6. GRANT PROGRAM

(a) AUTHORITY TO MAKE GRANTS—The Office of Justice Programs of the Department of Justice shall make grants, in accordance with such regulations as the Attorney General may prescribe, to State and local programs designed to combat hate crimes committed by juveniles, including programs to train local law enforcement officers in investigating, prosecuting, and preventing hate crimes.

(b) AUTHORIZATION OF APPROPRIATIONS—There are authorized to be appropriated such sums as may be necessary to carry out this section.

SEC. 7. AUTHORIZATION FOR ADDITIONAL PERSONNEL TO ASSIST STATE AND LOCAL LAW ENFORCEMENT

There are authorized to be appropriated to the Department of the Treasury and the Department of Justice, including the Community Relations Service, for fiscal years 2000, 2001, and 2002 such sums as are necessary to increase the number of personnel to prevent and respond to alleged violations of section 245 of title 18, United States Code (as amended by this Act).

SEC. 8. SEVERABILITY

If any provision of this Act, an amendment made by this Act, or the application of such provision or amendment to any person or circumstance is held to be unconstitutional, the remainder of this Act, the amendments made by this Act, and the application of the provisions of such to any person or circumstance shall not be affected thereby.

SUMMARY

HCPA amends current law. HCPA breaks no new ground. Since 1969, 18 U.S.C. Sec. 245 has permitted federal prosecution of a hate crime if the crime was motivated by bias based on race, religion, national origin, or color, and because the victim was exercising a "federally protected right" (e.g., voting, attending school, etc.). After thirty years, it has become clear that the statute needs to be amended. HCPA removes the federally protected activity requirement and adds actual or perceived sexual orientation, gender, and disability to the list of covered categories, thus bringing much needed uniformity to federal law.

HCPA would allow limited federal prosecution. There have never been more than ten prosecutions brought under 18 U.S.C. Sec. 245 in a single year. Since 1991, the FBI has documented over 50,000 hate crimes. During that six-year period, however, the Justice Department brought only thirty-seven cases under 18 U.S.C. Sec. 245. For the three new categories, HCPA only covers violent acts resulting in death or bodily injury and includes a constitutional requirement or commerce clause nexus—that the perpetrator or victim has traveled in interstate commerce or used the "facilities" of interstate commerce. The bill also includes a provision that the attorney general or his or her designee must certify, in writing, that a federal prosecution may go forward.

The federal government has a responsibility to ensure equal treatment. Since Reconstruction, federal law has barred certain egregious conduct because it is based on racial prejudice or other kinds of invidious discrimination. This federal role is based on the special constitutional responsibility placed on the federal government to ensure that no American citizen is subject to discriminatory treatment because of deep-seated prejudice. In addition to allowing the federal government to serve as an important backstop to state and local law enforcement, passage of HCPA would result in increased public education and awareness, more victims coming forward to report hate crimes, increased reporting by local law enforcement to the FBI under the Hate Crimes Statistics Act, and a clearer demonstration of the federal government's resolve to deal with violence based on prejudice. Passage of the act puts would-be perpetrators on notice that our society does not tolerate these kinds of criminal actions.

States will continue to play the primary role in combating violent crime. The vast majority of hate crimes will continue to be investigated and prosecuted at the state level. HCPA will provide a backstop to state and local law enforcement by allowing federal authorities to assist in investigations and to prosecute cases if and only if it is necessary to achieve an effective, just result. Currently, there is overlapping federal jurisdiction in the case of many homicides, bank robberies, kidnappings, fraud, and other crimes. As is frequently the case when federal and state laws overlap, only a fraction of cases subject to federal jurisdiction would result in actual federal prosecution.

The Senate has overwhelmingly supported similar federal hate crimes legislation. In 1996, the Senate voted 98 to 0 to pass the Church Arson Prevention Act, an amendment to 18 U.S.C. Sec. 247 that clarified the federal role in the investigation and prosecution of bias crimes based on ethnic or racial animus targeted at religious property. While HCPA does not cover property—only crimes against persons resulting in death or bodily injury—both amendments contain a commerce clause nexus, thus granting federal jurisdiction.

The American public supports federal hate crimes legislation. Public opinion polling consistently finds the overwhelming majority of Americans in support of inclusion of sexual orientation in federal hate crimes laws. An April 1999 poll conducted by Penn, Schoen, and Berland Associates[1] found that 91 percent of young people believe that hate crimes are a serious national problem, and 95 percent support expanding federal law to include sexual orientation, gender, and disability, which HCPA does.

Notes

Chapter 1

1. Stanley Coren. *The Left-Hander Syndrome: The Causes and Consequences of Left-Handedness* (New York: Free Press, 1992).

2. Hendrick Smith, "Teaching Tolerance—Confronting Discrimination, One Teen at a Time," *USA Weekend,* September 19, 1999, p. 4.

3. Dianne Carmen, "Justice Only Goes Halfway," *Denver Post,* November 4, 1999, Section B, p. 1.

4. Lisa Bennett, *Mixed Blessings: Mainstream Religion and Gay and Lesbian Americans*, Washington, DC: The HRC Foundation, Human Rights Campaign, 1999, <www.hrc.org>.

5. National Conference of Catholic Bishops, "Always Our Children—A Pastoral Message to Parents of Homosexual Children and Suggestions for Pastoral Ministers." Pastoral report, 1998, Internet source.

6. Chandler Burr, *A Separate Creation: The Search for the Biological Origins of Sexual Orientation* (New York: Hyperion, 1996).

7. Alfred C. Kinsey, Wardell B. Pomeroy, and Clyde E. Martin, *Sexual Behavior in the Human Male* (Philadelphia: W. B. Saunders Co., 1948).

8. Alfred C. Kinsey, Wardell B. Pomeroy, Clyde E. Martin, and Paul Gebhard, *Sex-ual Behavior in the Human Female* (Philadelphia: W. B. Saunders Co., 1953).

9. Dean Hamer, *The Science of Desire: The Search for the Gay Gene and the Biology of Behavior* (New York: Simon & Schuster, 1994); Simon LeVay, *The Sexual Brain* (Cambridge, MA: MIT Press, 1993).

10. Bruce Bagemihl, *Biological Exuberance: Animal Homosexuality and Natural Diversity* (New York: St. Martin's Press, 1998).

Chapter 2

1. Edward E. Hubbard, *Measuring Diversity Results, Volume 1.* (Petaluma, CA: Global Insights Publishing, 1997).

2. Louise Young, *State of the Workplace Report,* Washington, DC: The Human Rights Campaign, 1999, <www.hrc.org>.

3. Rosabeth Moss Kanter, *The Change Masters: Innovations for Productivity in the American Corporation* (New York: Simon & Schuster, 1983).

4. Grant Lukenbill, *The Gay and Lesbian Value Index,* GLVReports, New York, 1999, <www.glvreports.com>.

5. Young, *State of the Workplace Report.*

6. Ibid.

7. "Mulryan/Nash—Simmons Market Reasearch Report—Sexual Orientation and the Market," Overlooked Opinions, Chicago, 1998.

8. Ibid.

9. Billie Stanton, "Changing Shape of Family Life," *Denver Post,* November 26, 1999, Section B, p. 16.

10. Patty Henetz, "Statistics Paint a New Picture of Family Structure," *The Salt Lake Tribune,* May 28, 1998, <www.saltlaketribune.com>.

11. Zev Singer, "Census to Ask if You're Gay—Same-Sex Couples to be Counted in 2001." *Ottawa Citizen,* October 31, 1999, Section II, p. 45.

12. Shell Exploration and Production Company, *Diversity Performance Standard,* created by a cross-functional team from various business units' diversity action teams, 1999. Used with permission.

13. Ibid., p. 6.

14. Alan Yang, "From Wrongs to Rights: Public Opinion on Gay and Lesbian Americans Moves Toward Equality 1973-1999," National Gay and Lesbian Task Force, Washington, DC, 1999.

15. Ibid.

16. Alistar D. Williamson, "Is This the Right Time to Come Out?" *Harvard Business Review,* March, 1993, p. 43.

Chapter 3

1. Warren J. Blumenfeld. *Homophobia: How We All Pay the Price.* (Boston: Beacon Press, 1992), p. 67.

2. Cooper Thompson, "Visions," The Campaign to End Homophobia, P.O. Box 819, Cambridge, MA, 1990, p. 45.

3. Gregory Herek, Heterosexuals' Attitudes Towards Lesbians and Gay Men: Correlates and Gender Differences," *The Journal of Sex Research,* November 1998, pp. 45-48.

4. "Don't Ask, Don't Tell" report on *60 Minutes,* CBS, December 12, 1999.

5. Dan Hawes, "Capital Gains and Losses: A State by State Review of Gay, Lesbian, Bisexual, Trangender and HIV/AIDS related Legislation in 1999," National Gay and Lesbian Task Force, Washington, DC, 1999.

6. Lisa Bennett, *Mixed Blessings: Mainstream Religion and Gay and Lesbian Americans*, Washington, DC: The HRC Foundation, Human Rights Campaign, 1999, p. 17, <www.hrc.org>.

7. Janis Walworth and Liz Winfeld, "Transgendered Issues in the Workplace," in Liz Winfeld, *A Trainer's Guide to Training Tough Topics* (New York: AMACOM, 2000).

8. As of January 1, 2000.

9. "Gays in the Workplace," *Fortune Magazine,* December 1991, p. 58.

10. Paul Gebhard, *Sex Offenders, An Analysis of Types* (New York: Harper & Row, 1985).

Chapter 4

1. Michelangelo Signorile. *Queer in America: Sex, Media and the Closets of Power* (New York: Random House, 1993).
2. Jonathan Rauch, *The Wall Street Journal,* December 12, 1998.
3. Vivienne Cass, "Homosexual Identity Formation: A Theoretical Model," *Journal of Homosexuality, Volume 4,* 1979, pp. 17-23.
4. Office of Personnel Management, "Addressing Sexual Orientation Discrimination in Federal Civilian Employment," Washington, DC: Author, June 1999.
5. See Appendixes E and F.
6. Patricia Digh, "Well-Managed Employee Networks Add Business Value," Diversity Agenda, *HRMagazine,* August, 1997, pp. 1-4.
7. Adapted from "A Guide to Starting an Employee Group," Chicago: Out at Work (or Not), 1993.
8. Michelle Conlin, "Religion in the Workplace: The Growing Presence of Spirituality in Corporate America," *BusinessWeek Online,* November 1, 1999.
9. Ibid.
10. Ibid.
11. Parents and Friends of Lesbians and Gays, Washington, DC, <www.pflag.org>.

Chapter 5

1. "HIV/AIDS Education in the Workplace," a study by the New York Business Group on Health, New York, 1990.
2. Shari Caudron, "Valuing Differences Not the Same As Managing Diversity," *Personal Journal,* April 1993, p. 56.
3. A complete description of this education can be found in Liz Winfeld, *A Trainer's Guide to Training Tough Topics* (New York: AMACOM, 2000).
4. Ibid.
5. Sara Rynes and Benson Rosen, "Profiting from Others' Experience: A Diversity Training Checklist," *HRMagazine,* October 1994, pp. 22-23, 66-67.
6. Richard Williams and Liz Winfeld, "HIV/AIDS Education in the Workplace," in Liz Winfeld, *A Trainer's Guide to Training Tough Topics* (New York: AMACOM, 2000).

Chapter 6

1. Liz Winfeld/Common Ground, "A Complete List of Organizations with DPBs in the United States and Canada," Common Ground, 2000, <www.commongrnd.com>.
2. Billie Stanton, "Changing Shape of Family Life," *Denver Post,* November 26, 1999, Section B, p. 16.
3. "On the Job" News Brief, *Denver Post,* November 8, 1999, Section C, p. 1.
4. Society of Human Resources Management, "Human Resources Management, Issues and Trends," June 16, 1999, Alexandria, VA.

5. United States Chamber of Commerce, Washington, DC, 1992.
6. "Effective Employee Benefits," The Employee Benefits Reasearch Group, Washington, DC, 1992, <www.ebrg.org>.
7. Sample affidavits are provided in Appendixes B and D.

Chapter 7

1. *American Heritage Dictionary,* New Second College Edition (New York: Dell Publishing/New Laurel Edition, 1989).
2. Statistics, definitions, and other data from "Legal Marriage Primer" and "Quick Facts on Legal Marriage for Same-Sex Couples," by Demian, co-director, Partners Task Force, <www.buddybuddy.com>.
3. John Boswell, *Same-sex Unions in Premodern Europe* (New York: Villard Books, 1994).
4. Gilbert Zicklin "Legal Trials and Tribulations," in *On the Road to Same-Sex Marriage,* edited by Robert P. Cabaj and David W. Purcell. (San Francisco: Jossey-Bass, 1998), pp. 129-139.
5. From the "Legal Marriage Primer," by Demian, co-director, Partners Task Force, <www.buddybuddy.com>.
6. Billie Stanton, "Changing Shape of Family Life," *Denver Post,* November 26, 1999, Section B, p. 16.
7. Alan Yang, "From Wrongs to Rights: Public Opinion on Gay and Lesbian Americans Moves Towards Equality 1973-1999," National Gay and Lesbian Task Force, Washington, DC, 1999.
8. Michael S. Wald, "The Wald Report: Same-Sex Couples, Marriage, Families and Children," Stanford Law, Stanford University, 1999.

Chapter 8

1. Alistair D. Williamson, "Is This the Right Time to Come Out?" *Harvard Business Review,* March, 1993, p. 45.
2. Janis Walworth and Liz Winfeld, "Transgender Issues in the Workplace," in Liz Winfeld, *A Trainer's Guide to Training Tough Topics* (New York: AMACOM, 2000).

Appendix F

1. Human Rights Campaign Bi-Partisan Poll on Sexual Orientation—Lake, Snell, Perry, and Associates (Democrats) and American Viewpoint (Republicans). Human Rights Campaign, Washington, DC, 1999, <www.hrc.org>. (The HRC commissioned the study to American Viewpoints who then used Pern, Schoen, and Berland for data collection.)

Additional Readings

Print Sources

Aarons, Leroy. *Prayers for Bobby.* San Francisco: HarperSanFrancisco, 1995.

Bagemihl, Bruce. *Biological Exuberance: Animal Homosexuality and Natural Diversity.* New York: St. Martin's Press, 1998.

Berzon, Betty. *Positively Gay.* Updated and expanded edition. Foreword by Congressman Barney Frank. Berkeley: Celestial Arts, 1992.

Berzon, Betty. *Setting Them Straight.* New York: Viking Penguin, 1996.

Blumenfeld, Warren J., Ed. *Homophobia: How We All Pay the Price.* Boston: Beacon Press, 1992.

Blumenfeld, Warren and Diane Raymond. *Looking at Gay and Lesbian Life.* Updated and expanded ed. Boston: Beacon Press, 1993.

Boykin, Keith. *One More River to Cross: Black and Gay in America.* New York: Anchor Books, 1998.

Cabaj, Robert P. and David W. Purcell. *On the Road to Same-Sex Marriage.* San Francisco: Jossey Bass, 1997.

Davis, Kenneth. *Don't Know Much About: The Bible.* New York: Eagle Brook, 1998.

Duberman, Martin. *Stonewall.* New York: Dutton, 1993.

Eskeridge, William. *The Case for Same-Sex Marriage.* Boston: Alyson Publications, 1996.

Eskeridge, William. *Gaylaw: Challenging the Apartheid of the Closet.* Cambridge, MA: Harvard University Press, 1999.

Friskopp, Annette and Sharon Silverstein. *Straight Jobs Gay Lives.* New York: Scribner, 1995.

Helminiak, Daniel. *What the Bible Really Says About Homosexuality.* San Francisco: Alamo Square Press, 1994.

Hunter, Nan D., et al. *The Rights of Lesbians and Gay Men: The Basic ACLU Guide to a Gay Person's Rights.* New York: New Press, 1992.

Jennings, Kevin, Ed. *One Teacher in Ten—Gay and Lesbian Educators Tell Their Stories.* Boston: Alyson Publications, 1994.

Lukenbill, Grant. *Untold Millions: Secret Truths About Marketing to Gay and Lesbian Consumers.* Binghamton, NY: The Haworth Press, 1999.

Lukenbill, Grant. *Smart Spending, The Gay and Lesbian Guide to Socially Responsible Shopping and Investing.* Boston: Alyson Publications, 1999.

Mohr, Richard D. *A More Perfect Union: Why Straight America Must Stand Up for Gay Rights.* Boston: Beacon Press, 1994.

Nava, Michael. *Created Equal: Why Gay Rights Matter to America.* New York: St. Martin's Press, 1994.

Office of Personnel Management. "Addressing Sexual Orientation Discrimination in Federal Civilian Employment: A Guide to Employees' Rights," <www.opm. gov/er/address2/Guide01.htm>.

Rasi, Richard A. and Lourdes Rodriguez-Nogues, eds. *Out in the Workplace: The Pleasures and Perils of Coming Out on the Job.* Los Angeles: Alyson Publications, 1995.

Saks, Adrien and Wayne Curtis, eds. *Revelations: Gay Mens' Coming Out Stories,* Second Edition. Boston: Alyson, 1994.

Signorile, Michelangelo. *Outing Yourself: How to Come Out as Lesbian or Gay to Your Family, Friends, and Coworkers.* New York: Random House, 1995.

Sutton, Roger. *Hearing Us Out: Voices from the Gay and Lesbian Community.* Boston: Little, Brown, 1994.

Wald, Michael, S. *The Wald Report, Same-Sex Couples, Marriage, Families and Children.* Stanford Law, Stanford, CA, 1999.

Winfeld, Liz. *A Trainer's Guide to Training Tough Topics.* A collection of curriculums in difficult diversity areas including: sexual orientation, sexual harassment, workplace violence, HIV/AIDS, disabilities, multiculturalism, transgenderism, religion/spirituality, and measurement and accountability. Available from AMACOM in Spring 2000. Please e-mail: <common-ground@icolorado.com> or call (303) 838-1855 for more details.

> *Note:* A list of publications, city by city, dealing with sexual orientation in those cities is available on the Web at: <www.geocities.com/westhollywood/heights/7553/>.

Internet Sources

<www.buddybuddy.com>—Partners Task Force for Gay and Lesbian Couples is a national resource supporting the diverse community of committed gay and lesbian partners through a variety of media. The place to go for legal relationship (marriage and domestic partnership) information.

<www.common-grnd.com>—Common Ground is an education/consulting firm specializing in education focused on sexual orientation in the workplace and on domestic partner benefits. They offer a full range of consulting on these and all related workplace issues.

<www.equalityproject.org>—The Equality Project promotes and monitors corporate adherance to contemporary business standards on sexual orientation policy for gay and lesbian consumers, employees, and investors.

<www.gayscribe.com>—The utimate listing of gay and lesbian publications from around the world.

<www.glvreports.com>—Grant Lukenbill is president of GLVReports and Communications, New York, an independent consumer and investor information news service.

The GLV Rating Scale and System was originally created in 1995 by Grant Lukenbill in conjunction with financial advisor Howard Tharsing, president of V-Management, San Francisco, CA. The GLV Index is now a wholly owned information product published exclusively by GLVReports and Communications with input from numerous gay and lesbian community organizers.

<www.lambda.org> and <www.glad.org>—Our choices for legal information and advice relative to sexual orientation.

<www.pflag.org>—PFLAG is a national nonprofit organization with a membership of over 77,000 households and more than 425 affiliates worldwide. This vast grassroots network is developed, resourced, and serviced by the PFLAG national office, located in Washington, DC.

Parents, Families and Friends of Lesbians and Gays promotes the health and well-being of gay, lesbian, bisexual, and transgendered persons, their families and friends through: support, to cope with an adverse society; education, to enlighten an ill-informed public; and advocacy, to end discrimination and to secure equal civil rights. Parents, Families and Friends of Lesbians and Gays provides opportunity for dialogue about sexual orientation and gender identity, and acts to create a society that is healthy and respectful of human diversity.

<www.sldn.org>—The Servicemembers Legal Defense Network is the sole national legal aid and watchdog organization that assists servicemembers hurt by the "don't ask, don't tell, don't pursue" policy.

<www.trilliuminvest.com>—Your guide to socially responsible investing and activism.

<www.witeckcombs.com>—Witeck-Combs is a professional partnership committed to helping our clients match their strategic communications objectives with their business goals.

Index

Order Your Own Copy of
This Important Book for Your Personal Library!

STRAIGHT TALK ABOUT GAYS IN THE WORKPLACE
Second Edition

_____ in hardbound at $49.95 (ISBN: 1-56023-170-X)

_____ in softbound at $24.95 (ISBN: 1-56023-171-8)

COST OF BOOKS_____

OUTSIDE USA/CANADA/
MEXICO: ADD 20%_____

POSTAGE & HANDLING_____
(US: $4.00 for first book & $1.50
for each additional book
Outside US: $5.00 for first book
& $2.00 for each additional book)

SUBTOTAL_____

IN CANADA: ADD 7% GST_____

STATE TAX_____
(NY, OH & MN residents, please
add appropriate local sales tax)

FINAL TOTAL_____
(If paying in Canadian funds,
convert using the current
exchange rate. UNESCO
coupons welcome.)

☐ **BILL ME LATER:** ($5 service charge will be added)
(Bill-me option is good on US/Canada/Mexico orders only;
not good to jobbers, wholesalers, or subscription agencies.)

☐ Check here if billing address is different from
shipping address and attach purchase order and
billing address information.

Signature_____

☐ **PAYMENT ENCLOSED: $**_____

☐ **PLEASE CHARGE TO MY CREDIT CARD.**

☐ Visa   ☐ MasterCard   ☐ AmEx   ☐ Discover
☐ Diner's Club   ☐ Eurocard   ☐ JCB

Account # _____

Exp. Date _____

Signature _____

Prices in US dollars and subject to change without notice.

NAME _____

INSTITUTION _____

ADDRESS _____

CITY _____

STATE/ZIP _____

COUNTRY _____ COUNTY (NY residents only) _____

TEL _____ FAX _____

E-MAIL_____

May we use your e-mail address for confirmations and other types of information? ☐ Yes   ☐ No
We appreciate receiving your e-mail address and fax number. Haworth would like to e-mail or fax special
discount offers to you, as a preferred customer. **We will never share, rent, or exchange your e-mail
address or fax number.** We regard such actions as an invasion of your privacy.

Order From Your Local Bookstore or Directly From

The Haworth Press, Inc.

10 Alice Street, Binghamton, New York 13904-1580 • USA

TELEPHONE: 1-800-HAWORTH (1-800-429-6784) / Outside US/Canada: (607) 722-5857

FAX: 1-800-895-0582 / Outside US/Canada: (607) 772-6362

E-mail: getinfo@haworthpressinc.com

PLEASE PHOTOCOPY THIS FORM FOR YOUR PERSONAL USE.

www.HaworthPress.com

BOF00